ESL Phonics
for All Ages

Teacher's Guide
and Answer Pages for
Book One
Book Two
Book Three

Elizabeth Claire

Production: Rosemarie Horner, Kraig Obermiller and Elizabeth Claire
Audio Director: Gene Zerna
Cover Design: Elizabeth Claire
Cover Photo: Corbis Photos
Copy Editors: Nadine Simms and Adelaide Coles
Special Thanks to Dr. Marilyn Rosenthal

©2010, 2015 Eardley Publications

Virginia Beach, VA 23456
www.Elizabethclaire.com

Printed in the United States of America

ISBN: 978-0937630-26-6

ESL Phonics for All Ages
Teacher's Guide
and Answer Pages for
Book One, Book Two, and Book Three

Contents

Book One: Beginning Consonants

Book Two: Ending Consonants

Book Three: Consonant Clusters

About *ESL Phonics for All Ages*

Who is it for?

ESL Phonics for All Ages is a program designed for students with the special needs of beginning English language learners (ELLs) in elementary years through adult. The **Student Books** are written with the presumption that students may know very little English, can not yet read in English, or perhaps can not read in any language.

The special accommodations to English language learners provide a good approach for native English speakers as well.

The multi-skills approach of *ESL Phonics for All Ages* enables a teacher to use the program with beginning classes in which some students require phonics instruction while others may need vocabulary building, spelling, pronunciation, and familiarity with sentence patterns.

Individual students can make rapid progress independently with the **Audio Program** and get instant feedback as they correct their own work with the **Answer Pages**.

Components

Six 96-page Student Books:

- **Book One**: Beginning Consonants

- **Book Two**: Ending Consonants

- **Book Three**: Consonant Clusters

- **Book Four**: Long Vowels and Digraphs

- **Book Five**: Short Vowels

- **Book Six**: Building Words (forthcoming)

- **Twelve Audio CDs** (Two per book)

- **Music CD**: Easy Songs for English Language Learners

- **A Teacher's Guide** to Books One, Two, and Three with Answer Pages.

Why do English language learners need a special approach to phonics?

English language learners will make much faster progress in learning to read when working with linguistically appropriate materials. It is frustrating both for newcomers and their teachers to use phonics materials designed for native speakers of English. These are inefficient at best, and are often demoralizing.

It makes good sense to teach a person to read first in his or her native language—many of the skills transfer readily. However, in many cases, this is just not practical. Students may not have the luxury of bilingual instruction, or they may come from cultures that do not have a tradition of literacy.

Here are just a few of the obvious reasons for needing special approaches to phonics:

1. **New English language learners have a very small store of words to draw on.**

    They are not likely to know the English names of things pictured in phonics books for native English speakers. Words such as *mat, vat, van, jug, tug, bud, cob,* and *bib* are not in their vocabulary. Words such as these are not only not known, they are not useful to a beginning speaker of English. Teacher time is required to explain these words. It is more efficient to teach students to read using a high percentage of words they already know or need to know.

2. **ELLs need everything at once:** vocabulary building, phonics, spelling, reading, writing, and conversation.

    Phonics books that limit the learning to a single sound, without presenting words in useful contexts, are not efficient.

3. **Pictures that refer to adjectives or verbs can cause confusion to English learners.**

    For example, to illustrate the word *slow*, a phonics book for native speakers may have a picture of a turtle. The beginning English language learner who does not know either the word *slow* or *turtle*, may assume that *slow* is the name of the animal. In a similar manner, a picture of a dog digging a hole, to illustrate the word *dig*, may create the misconception that the spelling of the word *dog* is **d-i-g**.

4. **New speakers of English can't hear English sounds that do not exist in their own language.**

    For example, a Hispanic student may not be able to discriminate between /ch/ and /sh/. Japanese and Chinese don't distinguish between /l/ and /r/. Vietnamese don't distinguish between /b/ and/p/. Filipinos don't distinguish between /f/ and /p/. This makes it difficult to associate a symbol with its correct sound.

    This is a small problem with a few consonants, but it is multiplied enormously with English vowel sounds (*kit, kite, Kate, cat, cot, cut, court, caught, coot, coat,* for example). Students from most other languages have difficulty discriminating these English sounds aurally, and even more difficulty in producing them.

5. **The sequence of reading skills for English language learners is different from sequences suitable for native English speakers.**

Typically, native English speakers begin their phonemic awareness with listening practice and rhyming words and then children are asked to generate words that begin with a particular sound. This is fine for English-speaking kindergartners. But these exercises are of a very high order of difficulty for beginning speakers of English. ELLs cannot generate vocabulary for beginning sounds as their vocabulary is extremely limited, and their ears not attuned yet to English sounds. ELLs may hear and pronounce *hot* and *cat* as rhyming words. Discriminating such closely related sounds is a more advanced activity for them, not a pre-reading activity.

In spite of a misconception that ABCs come first, new readers do not need to learn all the letters of the alphabet, capital and lower case before the first reading lesson. In fact, that easily overwhelms a student without motivating him or her to connect the letters with sounds and real words and meanings. Learning just a few letters at a time will do. Capital letters are presented only as needed, one-by-one.

There is no harm in learning to sing the alphabet song. However, learning to distinguish, identify, and write the entire alphabet upper and lower case, is not a prerequisite for beginning phonics instruction.

6. **Sentence structures for practice**

reading are more effective when they parallel the structures being taught in the students' ESL classes.

It's easier to learn to read sentences that reflect general conversation heard in the ESL learner's environment, or beginning lessons in the ESL class. Phonics books for native English speakers can properly use artificial sentences such as *The fat cat sat on a mat* to illustrate a phonics concept. However, for an English language learner, there is less value in learning to read or say such sentences, as they fill no need in conversation or writing in the reader's life, and tend to trivialize the purpose and outcome of reading.

Besides, all those three-letter words look alike to a language learner. The language learners brain does better when words have a variety of distinct shapes from each other.

7. **ELLs need grammatically correct and useful sentences in their practice reading.**

The reading practice in many beginning native English phonics books is stilted and unnatural. For example, one phonics book uses many sentences of the pattern: *The cat runs to Jim.* This is a misuse of the simple present tense. The present tense of the verb implies a regular, repeated daily action.

For English learners, this stilted construction interferes with learning the appropriate situations for using the present tense forms of verbs. (Native English writers and speakers, except in photo captions, do not use the present tense form of verbs when identifying actions in pictures.) The present continuous tense is more natural: *The cat is running to Jim.*

Writers of phonics materials for native English speakers can justify this practice of mismatching verb tenses, but phonics materials for new speakers of English should not introduce incorrect sentence patterns.

Another example in native English phonics books are sentences such as *The pup wags, The hens tug.* The verbs *wag* and *tug* are transitive, and in natural, standard English, there is an obligatory direct object to follow the verb.

This is not a problem for native English speakers who won't be influenced by the grammatical weirdness. However, leaving the direct object out of the sentence is not OK for English learners, as it teaches poor structure (and assuming that the student can figure out the meaning of *hen, pup, tug,* and *wag* from the pictures).

8. **English language learners need success, not frustration. They need challenges within their limited ability to make distinctions.**

In a native English speakers' phonics book, the student may be asked to choose the best word in sentences such as *The dog _____ to Jim.* (*run, runs*). First-year English learners have not incorporated the notion that the singular noun requires the third person present tense marker, as in *runs*. (Nor is the sentence an accurate reflection

of standard English usage.) Phonics for English language learners should avoid setting up wrong patterns (and later confusion) by such examples.

9. **New speakers of English continue to need clear illustrations, consistent instructions, and simple sentence structures throughout the presentation of phonics elements.**

Typical native English speakers' phonics workbooks use abstract ideas, and many idiomatic sentence structures. A page that would take a native English-speaking student three minutes or less to complete may require a half hour of one-to-one teacher time to instruct English language learners in vocabulary, context, sounds, idiomatic structures, cultural background, and other concepts.

10. **Language learners need audio input.**

Teachers need a program in which the pre-literate ESL student can progress at his or her own pace without the constant dependence on a teacher for hearing the sounds of words.

How does ESL Phonics for All Ages meet the needs of English Language Learners?

- **Directions are simple and repetitive.** This allows students to proceed with confidence with aural input from teacher, tutor, classroom buddy, or the audio CD.

- **Instructions are clear and easy to follow**. After a few sample lessons with a teacher, students can work at their own pace using the audio CDs.

They will easily learn the English instructions with icons to remind them of their meanings.

- **Useful, everyday concrete vocabulary is developed.** Students will recognize words they need to know or already know. *ESL Phonics for All Ages* does not limit itself to three-letter words, but uses words that are needed and useful to first year English language learners. There are 340 words in **Book One**. Three hundred are concrete nouns, accompanied by simple black line illustrations. Forty verbs and common function words are used both in instructions and in practice sentences.

- **CDs provide audio input.** Every word is pronounced three times in the presentation of each new sound/symbol correspondence. Each sentence is read at slow-normal speed with appropriate intonation, and with time for the student to repeat the sentence. A variety of voices enhances exposure to standard English. Cheerful bridge music keeps students alert and helps clarify when activities begin and end.

- **Illustrations are realistic and non-juvenile.** These books may be used without embarrassment by students of any age.

- **Students encounter the complete spellings of all words.** As the student listens for the phonics element being taught, he or she sees the complete word, forming a foundation for later spelling competency.

- **Vocabulary is used in sentence patterns typical of basic first-year ESL lessons.** These sentence patterns are repeated much as they might be in English lessons for beginners. *ESL Phonics for All Ages* reinforces the lessons learned in ESL class and avoids the non-useful sentences often found in phonics for English speakers. Important sight words are taught in context. This whole-language approach assists students in acquiring language they can use every day.

- **Songs and chants engage the right brain in learning.** Traditional simple songs, poems, and chants provide fun and teach a bit of American culture while assisting reading success.

- **The *ESL Phonics for All Ages* program capitalizes on the vastly complex abilities of the brain.** It taps into many possible learner strategies for learning to read: phonics, sight words, rote learning, repetition, using visuals as clues to allow for guessing, chants and songs for memorization and right-brain learning, and the sense of success and progress that encourage each student.

- **Lessons are multi-level.** Student interest is kept up with vocabulary building, spelling, and meaningful whole language. By spelling out full words when only the beginning sounds are focused on, we allow the learner to generate hypotheses about symbols and sounds. This allows the learner to experience the "Ah hah!" phenomenon over and over and over. This subjective "Ah hah!" that the student says to him or herself is a reward, a jolt of juice. It's a great motivator. It validates to the student what he or she has hypothesized, or rewards the student with an answer to a puzzle the mind has placed in waiting.

- **Students check their own work.** Students don't need to wait for the teacher to provide input or feedback, but can get that within a few minutes of completing each activity. They get non-judgmental feedback from correcting their own mistakes, and reinforcement from seeing the speed of their progress.

- **Student success is what it's all about.** Lessons are designed so students can progress through presentation, production and practice, self-testing, and self-correction and feedback for maximum success.

How much English must a student know before beginning to read?

Some researchers recommend that a student be adequately proficient in English before formal reading instruction. In the meantime, instruction in reading should begin or continue in the native language.

However, with an approach that includes controlled high-frequency vocabulary, simple structures, careful sound-sequencing and meaningful reading as well as aural input and vocabulary development, reading instruction in English can proceed quite early in an English language learner's education—much earlier than if you are using phonics materials for English speakers. In fact, our experience shows that delaying effective reading instruction in English increases a student's anxiety, while providing for success in reading creates confidence and progress.

How is *ESL Phonics for All Ages* sequenced?

The organization of the series is designed specifically for the needs of English language learners. Sound/symbols are sequenced from least difficult to more difficult. Consonants present much less difficulty than short vowels, for example. Contrasting consonants that are far apart visually and aurally (example, **b** and **t**; **s** and **n**) allows learners to easily grasp the difference through sight and sound.

ESL Phonics for All Ages focuses on consonant sounds in the first three Student Books, before requiring students to distinguish the more difficult English vowel sounds and their inconsistent spellings (presented in Books Four and Five).

Book One introduces 340 high-frequency words in the presentation of twenty initial consonants.

Book Two presents twenty-two final consonant sounds and their spellings in 190 additional new words.

Book Three presents consonant clusters in initial, middle, and final word position and introduces another 310 new words.

Book Four presents long vowels and digraphs.

Book Five presents short vowels and r-influenced vowels.

Book Six: *Building Words* presents contractions, prefixes and suffixes, compound words, and homonyms.

Books Four, Five, and Six build on previously learned sound/symbol awareness, reviewing many previous words and introducing additional useful words.

The sentence patterns in all of the books are short and at a beginners' level.

Books Two, Three, Four, and Five include short stories.

What grade level does each Student Book correspond to?

Students from first grade through high school and adults can learn phonics with our series.

The scope of this series is to have the student master decoding at a second grade level. This will prepare students to switch from learning to read to reading to learn. Students will be able to achieve different grade levels in reading depending on their current vocabulary development and their understanding of spoken English.

How is decoding different from reading?

Decoding is the ability to accurately sound-out words in a language when looking at written symbols. Decoding is not reading.

Accurate and efficient decoding is the basis for skills in reading. However, reading comprehension is much more than mere decoding.

Reading comprehension also depends on:

* an understanding of the meanings of the words, idioms, and context of a passage

* familiarity with simple and complex sentence structures

* the density of unknown vocabulary

* the age-appropriateness of the topic

* the student's interpretive skills and cultural awareness

For example, an English language learner may learn to accurately decode and speak aloud a sentence such as:

Individuals suffering from hyperventilation can alleviate their anxiety by breathing into a paper bag.

But unless all these words are in the student's passive vocabulary, the students won't absorb meaning from the words, so it is not true reading even if it "sounds like it." A reading grade level implies a knowledge of a certain volume of vocabulary. This is more than the competent learner may have acquired, even if he or she can accurately decode words.

In fact, teachers should be aware of "false reading" by students who have become good at decoding and pronunciation. Students may be able to decode advanced texts without understanding the vocabulary and content.

The *ESL Phonics for All Ages* program paves the way for the student to face elementary textbooks with courage and enjoy reading simple books for pleasure. The best way to continue to learn reading skills is to read interesting books at a suitable level.

How rapidly will a student progress?

Students who have used this program have developed decoding skills with greater efficiency and speed, and less frustration compared with other phonics programs. It is nevertheless impossible to predict how rapidly a particular student will progress.

Every student is unique. The variables of age, level of English comprehension, native-language literacy, motivation and other affective factors, family factors and time spent on task are too great to measure one English learner against another.

We do know that the progress of any student using this program will be optimal when you support the student in working at his or her own pace, supplying support and encouragement, and not in competition with others.

At the beginning

First must come the student's insight that marks on a page can represent sounds, and that these marks are put together to form words, and that words can be orally or mentally recreated by a process we call reading. Parents and teachers traditionally promote this insight by reading enjoyable stories to their children or students, and by providing printed words for the student's own name, and classmates' names, labels for things in the classroom and environmental print, such as street signs and names of familiar products and brands.

Foster a desire to read

Desire plays a strong part in success, because desire precedes attention. Success fuels desire, and desire fuels attention and further success. Relationships with fellow students and with teachers are key ingredients. When a student feels valued, feels successful, and recognizes the usefulness of content to him or her, reading will happen faster than if those circumstances are missing.

Once the first insight—that symbols can represent sounds and can be decoded—is understood, then the brain is capable of applying myriads of learning strategies and techniques if the desire to read is present.

Read to the students

Have other readers read to them. Choose highly illustrated books with action plots, and likeable characters suitable for your students' ages. Point to the characters and objects as you mention them, to make the story comprehensible. Read the same story several times.

Meaning and purpose for reading must be included from the start, not delayed until the student is allegedly ready to put it all together.

Language Experience Activities

Language Experience Activities work like this: Students do something interesting. While in action, they learn to understand, and then use, the vocabulary and structures they need to do the activity. Later, students retell the experience, and watch, as you write down their words on a large chart or board. Say each word as you write it. Then read their sentences back, pointing to the words as you say them.

These language experience activities are a vital part of learning to read. The experience in the classroom can be as simple as talking about what's new for an adult class and writing what they say. Other examples of interesting language experience activities are making popcorn or a fruit salad, setting the table, taking a walk, making introductions, visiting the nurse, and so forth, depending on the needs of your students. (For 160 language learning activities, see my *ESL Teacher's Activities Kit*, Eardley Publications.)

Songs, chants, dialogs, and other memorized material

Present a song, poem, or chant aurally yourself, or through a recording. Use pictures and actions to make the meaning comprehensible. Spend five or six minutes on this activity, and on following days, repeat the song or chant several times. When students feel capable, encourage them to chant or sing along with the CD or with you.

Don't present the written form until the auditory memory has been "primed" and the students know the song by heart.

Present the words to the song on a large chart paper or on the board. Teach left-to-right progression by pointing to each word as you sing it or say it. Say a line, and have students then read the line, using their memory of the song to clue their reading. Have individuals come up to the board to point to the words and read them.

Phonics vs. Sight reading

The education establishment has fought over methodologies for teaching reading to native English speakers for many decades. The pendulum has swung from phonics to sight reading and whole language to combinations of these and back again. The research on what works with non-native speakers is quite sparse and non-conclusive. Our pre-literate students are of such a variety of ages, backgrounds, English abilities, intelligence, cultures, previous educational histories, and home situations that mass comparisons of methods aren't statistically valid as yet.

What's happening inside a new readers' mind?

Researchers cannot cut open the mind and watch the process of learning to read,

But there are lots of theories. Most adults do not remember the specifics of how they learned to read. Different people seem to learn to read differently, so with the wide variety of students in our classes, we need a variety of teaching strategies and techniques. We must conclude that the human brain is just as mysteriously wired for decoding and understanding written symbols as it is wired to decode and understand auditory symbols. We teachers have to tap into that wiring by providing clues in the forms and at a pace that will lead to an enjoyable challenge and success.

We can observe what works, but not exactly how it works. The mind seems to operate on a quantum-particle level of energy bursts and electron storage. We can eventually input the combinations of symbolic markings—if attention is directed to them. We assemble them to assign meanings and memories. This allows

us to read at a speed far greater than would be allowed by phonetic sounding-out of words alone.

Reading research surprises

There has been a popular message from research being repeatedly printed and sent around the Internet. Most native born adult literate English speakers can easily read it. Perhaps you can, too.

Sicnetsts haev fnoud taht popele can raed much fsaetr tahn wluod be epxtced form mrleey uinsg phentoics. Yuo can raed tihs becuase the biran prcosses wrdos by the frsit and lsat lttres and not thurogh snuodnig out phnotcaeliy.

Waht is srupisirng is taht eevn stnuetds who have lraeend to raed Egnilsh as a sceond lgnuaage can raed thsee setnecetns.

Ijn addibtion, wze cabn throqw a looase lettcer indto worwds anzd fifnd thamt realding doeys nogt sujffer vdery muach.

eW nac esrever eht redro fo srettel dna dnif doog sredaer gniwolf hguorht eht txet sa ylisae.

.begin to where know they once trouble little have They .easily text the through flowing readers find and words of order the reverse can We

Your Class

Every class with new readers is different. If you have a group of students of similar abilities in English, you can use the teaching strategies in this book to expand oral production and practice in speaking as well as present the phonics.

If your class is more typical and has some students who can already read English, others who can read in their native language but not yet in English, and a few who cannot read in any language, you'll need to allow students to learn at their own pace.

Students with a good aural understanding and at least an intermediate vocabulary won't need external aural input. They will likely know most of the words, and can verbalize them to themselves softly.

Students who are new to English, and have very limited vocabulary will need audio input from CDs or a tutor, so they can learn the words for the pictured items. The audio CDs fulfill that need by reading the instructions to the student, and reading each word three times.

Getting Started

1. Be sure the student has a sharpened pencil and a good eraser. Notice how the student holds the pencil. Help younger students learn an efficient way to hold a pencil. Don't presume a student is right-handed, but see which hand he or she picks things up with. Provide demonstration for whichever hand students favor.

Older students may have developed an unusual way of holding a pencil, and the habit is ingrained. After a few demonstrations, if a student is effective with his or her preferred way of holding the pen, do not interfere.

2. Review the sounds of the numerals one to twenty to be sure the student recognizes them when he or she hears them.

3. Introduce the book simply saying, "This book will help you learn to read."

4. Use gestures and demonstrations to convey the your instructions to the student. Point to things as needed.

5. The icons on page one of each book help students learn what to do. Go over these icons so students understand the meaning. Use gestures to make the action comprehensible. Point to each icon and each word as you read it.

6. The headings for each of the activities also function as the directions to the student. The headings are in simple, active, imperative sentences.

Assuring Success

7. Pay careful attention to the presentation of the first lessons in the book, and to assure that the student understands what to do, how to write the letters, how to correct the challenge pages, and how to track their results. You want the student to be successful, and to know that you are not turning him or her loose on their own, but will be monitoring their progress.

8. Early success is very important. Don't take anything for granted, from turning pages, to moving from left to right, top to bottom, to operating the CD player or computer, to holding a pencil.

9. Show the student how to stop and start the CD player, and raise a hand to ask for help. Show him or her how to go back, repeat, or skip to the next track needed.

10. Give the student a set of **Answer Pages** (these may be photocopied) and demonstrate how to correct her or his own work. Monitor the first lessons until the student feels comfortable and demonstrates success in working on his or her own with the audio. Assure that the student is successful and accurate about self-checking, and understands what to do. You want the student to enjoy the time spent with the CD and the **Student Books**.

11. If your student makes errors, work with him or her carefully to diagnose difficulties, whether it be in visual discrimination, audio discrimination, motivation, or attention. Don't be hasty in diagnosing a learning disorder. Vision tests and audio tests may be called for. Speak more slowly, repeat lessons, or work in shorter sessions, if necessary.

12. If the student has a CD player at home (or your school media center lends them out) allow the student to take the book and the CD home if he or she seems eager to do so.

13. On pages such as "**Read and Draw**" or "**Read and Find**" where audio input is not given, the student will hear the instructions on the audio and about 15 seconds of music. Demonstrate to the student how to pause the CD player and complete the activity. Then resume the CD, check his or her work, and continue with the next activity.

14. Don't leave student isolated with the CD player for more than 30 minutes at a time. Have the student participate as much as possible in class lessons and create a place for him/herself in the social interactions.

Directions to the Student

The headings at the top of each page of activities function as the directions to the student. The headings are in simple, active, imperative sentences. When you present a lesson (for example,

Listen, Say, and Write),

read the heading, point to each icon, and give the aural input required on the page.

This type of activity introduces new sound/symbol correspondences. Students may learn new words at the same time. Students should write the missing letter as they say the word so listening, speaking, doing, and connecting are all going on.

1. Have the students watch your mouth as you say a new letter and its sound. Exaggerate the formation of the sound, for example, the explosion of the /b/ sound, or extend the duration of the /m/ or /s/ sound. Say each sound and word three times or more.

2. Point to the first picture as you say it, then point to the word, and say the word again. Exaggerate the initial sound.

3. Have the students say the word. It may help to provide hand mirrors so students can watch the position of their lips, teeth, and tongue as they make the sound.

4. DO NOT stress perfect pronunciation for beginning students at this point. Pronunciation is a very different skill. Phonics is about aural recognition of sounds and their symbols, not about perfect oral production.

5. Have students write the new letter(s) on the line for the sound(s) in each word. They don't have to write the entire word or learn how to spell it.

6. Give feedback immediately. Be enthusiastic in your appreciation of the students' accomplishments. Say, "That's right," "Good," and other affirming comments. Use English!

7. After the student completes a page, check his or her recognition of the items pictured: Say a word and have the student point to it. Don't require that the student name a picture you point to—recognition is adequate learning at this stage. Praise success.

Challenge Pages

On these pages, students test themselves in their ability to distinguish between the two new sounds just practiced. The challenge page asks students to write missing letter as they listen to each word.

Give the student the appropriate **Answer Pages**, and show him or her how to check his or her answers (example: a large C for correct, and an X for error). Show students where to enter the number of correct answers for the challenge page on right line of the tracking page at the back of each book.

On a later day, check for student recognition of the vocabulary. Call out the words on the page at random and have students either point to the picture of that word or say the number of the picture. Don't forget the praise for recognition.

When recognition is successful, check the students' ability to recall the names for the pictures.

What else?

It cannot be stressed too much or too often that phonics is one of the tools, but not the goal.

Students need to engage in activities that involve meaningful and pleasurable reading before, during, and after phonics instruction. There need to be books available to students in English and in their home language, and story-telling time, with easy-to-understand, action-based, well-illustrated books. Students need to be surrounded by captioned pictures, environmental print, and other comprehensible reading opportunities.

The student's anxiety over the inability to read needs to be replaced with confidence that reading will be possible. Confidence is a key ingredient for rapid progress. Build your student's confidence by tailoring each lesson a step above the student's current ability—just enough to be a challenge, but at a level at which he or she is likely to succeed. Follow the success with acknowledgment and praise.

Students who feel smart learn faster!

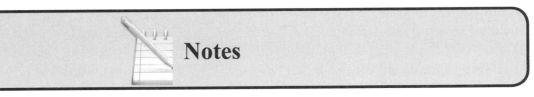

Types of Activities in the Student Book

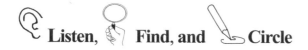

Listen, **Find, and** **Circle**

Visual discrimination: The student is challenged to find a word in a row of words that matches a pictured word on the left. In other versions of this activity, the student is challenged to find two words alike in a row of words.

1. Read the directions to the student.

2. Then read the first item and say the name of the word as you point to it.

3. Point to the circle around the word that is the same. (Here, the student is reviewing names of things as well as learning the English instructions *Draw a circle*, *same word*, and so forth.) The student draws a circle around the word that appears the same.

4. Give immediate feedback, and either coach or praise, as necessary.

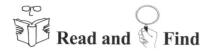

Read and **Find**

This activity type challenges a student to read a sentence and match it to a picture. This activity includes sight words in useful sentences. There is no audio input here. The sentences use simple structures that reinforce structures encountered in a beginning ESL class.

1. Read the first sentence and ask the student to point to the picture that corresponds with it. Demonstrate "draw a line" from each sentence to the picture it represents.

2. Allow the student to turn back to a previous page to get the correct answer, if necessary.

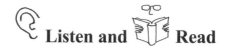

Listen and **Read**

Give audio input or have the student listen as the CD reads the sentences or conversations. Audio support gives the rhythm and intonation of basic question and answer patterns used in English.

For example, in **Book Two**, Unit Six, *Can you fix my ring?, No, sorry, I can't fix your ring, Can you fix my clock?, No, sorry, I can't fix your clock.* Many of these conversations have students focus on the sounds and vocabulary they have previously learned, and now encounter them with additional sight words in highly useful sentences, questions, and answers.

Function words, verbs, and important sight words are introduced. These are best learned by sight, since many of them are not phonetically regular.

1. If the students have little or no English at all, use puppets to act out conversations to teach the sounds, rhythms, and meanings of the sentences orally. Use objects, pictures, and gestures to make the sentences comprehensible.

2. Read the sentences and have the students repeat after you as they point to the words that they are saying.

3. Say the sentences at random and have students tell you the number of the sentence you have read.

4. Have students read in pairs. Demonstrate and encourage reading with enthusiasm, as if acting out their sentences or questions and answers in a conversational style.

👂 Listen, 📖 Read, and 🎵 Sing

This activity provides a text that students have already memorized. Students can draw on their right-brain memory of the words in the song as clues to the sounds of the words they see in the text.

1. Play the CD *Easy Songs for English Language Learners* in the background for some time each day.

2. Teach the song for oral production without reference to the written text. Clarify vocabulary through pictures, actions, and gestures.

3. Have students sing along with the CD, or with you, for several days until they know the song by heart. Review the songs from time to time.

4. After students are able to sing along with you, write the words to the song on a large chart paper or on the board.

5. Sing the song slowly as you point to each word. You are demonstrating left to right progression of reading, which is a key insight and skill for beginning readers.

6. Then read the song as you point to the words and have students repeat after you.

7. Have a student come to the board to point to the words as you say them in order.

8. Point to a key word that is repeated in the song, as you say it. Ask, "Can you find another_____ (whatever the word is)? How many (words) can you see?" Do the same with other key words. Ask, "What letter does _____ begin with?"

9. Point to the upper case and lower case letters of the same letter. For example, teach capital (**B**) and small (**b**). Have students point to words that begin with this letter, and read them or you read them. Have students find all instances of words that begin with that letter.

10. Ask questions about other key words. Ask, "What letter does _____ begin with? What letter does _____ end with?"

11. If there are rhyming words in the song, point them out to the students. Have them repeat the rhyming words and say, "These words rhyme." Suggest other words that rhyme with the words in the song.

12. Write each line of the song on a sentence strip. Hold the strips up one at a time, in order, for students to read after you.

13. Cut the strip into pieces with one word on each piece. Shuffle the pieces. Have a student put the words back into the correct order. (You might leave the written text with the correct order of words on the board for students to consult when they first put the words back into sentence order.)

14. With students in upper grades, also

cut out the punctuation, and teach the words *comma, period, question mark,* and *exclamation point,* as needed.

15. Use a ruler to draw straight dotted cutting lines between each of the lines of the song. Make photocopies. Have students cut the song into several strips, and mix them up. Then ask them to put the lines back into correct order. They will use a variety of clues, including phonics awareness to do this.

16. On another day, write the song on the board again. Have students read it aloud together as you say it. Have students close their eyes. Erase one word. Write a star in its place. Have students open their eyes. Can they tell you which word is missing? Have students read the sentence and say the missing word. Repeat this until no words are left on the board and students are singing "the stars."

17. Make flash cards with each word in the song to practice instant recognition.

 Chant or Poem

Chants, like songs, engage the right brain. Chants reinforce pronunciation as well as the natural rhythm and intonation of the language. Chants are a fun way to help promote reading success.

1. Present the chant for aural familiarity and comprehension in advance of using it as a reading activity.

2. Clarify the meaning of new words in the chant through pictures, actions, and gestures.

3. After students can say the chant by heart, write the words on the board or on large chart paper in large print.

4. Read the words as you point to them. Use dramatic, expressive intonation.

5. Read the words in order. Have a student point to each word as you read it.

6. Say the words at random and have a student point to them. Say, "Find a word that begins with (**b_**); with (**t_**)."

7. Prepare a sentence strip for each line of the chant or poem. Have students put the strips in the correct order. You can leave the original written form on the board for students to consult.

8. Cut the strips into pieces and have students put the pieces together to recreate the poem or chant.

9. Make enough photocopies of the chant for the students. Have each student cut the chant into strips, and then cut each strip into the individual words. Have them mix the words up and then recreate the chant by taping or pasting the words in correct order on a sheet of paper. Have the example on the board for students to match if necessary.

10. On another day, write the poem or chant on the board again. Have students read it together as you say it.

11. As you did with the song, have students close their eyes as you erase one word from the chant, and draw a star in its place. Then have students "chant the stars."

 **Conversation**

Many of the sentence patterns in various activity types throughout the **Student Books** lend themselves to short conversations.

1. Use two hand puppets to demonstrate the conversation between two people. Use an exaggerated intonation and rhythm. Clarify meanings through gestures, actions, and pictures.

2. Repeat the conversation until students know it by heart. Have students make paper hand puppets of their own and create the conversation.

3. Have students come in front of the class to act out the conversation from memory, ad-libbing when necessary, with the English that is available to them.

4. Write out the conversation on the board or on chart paper with the words of the first person on the left, and the second person on the right.

5. Divide the class into two groups, the first group takes the part of the first person, and the second group takes the part of the second person.

6. Have each group read only its part of the conversation after you.

7. Then have students switch, so they are reading the other side of the conversation.

8. Prepare sentence strips of the

conversation, and have students put them back in order.

 **Read and** **Draw**

The **Read and Draw** pages were added to **Book One** by the request of younger children working with the book.

Show students how to quickly make stick figures to illustrate the sentences to show they can read with understanding.

Skip this activity if drawing is frustrating or not appropriate for your students. On the other hand, check the work of those who have drawn pictures to verify that they have illustrated sentences correctly.

Listen and **Read the Story**

Stories appear at the end of **Book Two** and in later books. The stories vary from two to four pages in length and students may know these Aesop's stories in their native language.

The stories provide a whole language context and an engaging reason to read, while reinforcing phonics concepts students have learned. The stories help develop fluency in reading and introduce new vocabulary in context.

1. Read the story to the students or have them listen to the audio CD. As students listen, have them point to the panel of the story that they hear and track the sentences with their fingers. In a second reading, you can have the students repeat each sentence as you read.

2. Present the new vocabulary in the story through gestures, actions, or pictures.

3. Say one of the sentences on a page at random and have students tell you the number of the panel it is in.

4. Have individual students read aloud, assisting if needed.

5. Have students take turns in pairs or groups, each reading a panel of the story.

6. Prepare a sentence strip for each panel. Have various students each hold a strip and then physically organize themselves in the actual sequence of the story. Each student reads his or her sentence in correct sequence.

7. Explain the procedures for the story activities. Have students do them individually or in pairs, allowing them to go back to check answers in the story. Assist as necessary.

8. Have students take the parts of the characters and act out the story.

9. Discuss the meaning of the proverb or adage that the story illustrates. Ask students to compare these with proverbs or sayings in their home country.

Mastery Tests and Reviews

The **Test** and/or **Review** pages in the various books of *ESL Phonics for All Ages* are different, depending on the needs of students at different language levels.

In **Book One**, the **Mastery Tests** on pages 86 through 89 are labeled "**Look and Write.**" These tests review the beginning consonants and vocabulary taught throughout the book and have no audio input. Students are cued only by a picture and have to write the missing letters at the beginning of each word.

In **Book Two**, the **Mastery Tests** on pages 80 through 89 are labeled "**Read and Write.**" Students identify and copy the appropriate words from a word box to match the pictures. They demonstrate their mastery of ending consonants and vocabulary. There is no audio input here.

The **Reviews** in **Books Two** and **Three** are accompanied by audio input on the CD.

The **Mastery Tests** can serve as a placement test prior to beginning an individualized program. A score of 90% or better on the **Mastery Test** at the end of **Book One** would indicate that a student could skip that book, for example, and move on to **Book Two**. A score of less than 70% would indicate that it would benefit the student to start with **Book One**. The same formula can be applied to **Book Two**, going to **Book Three**. The **Review Tests** in **Book Three** can indicate the progress of the student.

Word Lists

At the back of each **Student Book**, there is a comprehensive list of the new words that appear in that book. There are many activities that can be done with the **Word Lists**. Here are a few:

1. Have students read the list with the help of a buddy, and with a pencil, check the words they can read, and circle the ones that are difficult.

2. Select twenty words at random for spelling tests, where the beginning students have merely to write the beginning letter. Advanced students can spell out the entire word.

3. Create flash cards of the words the student needs practice with on 3 x 5 cards or smaller cards. Have a student work with a buddy to practice sight-reading / sounding-out the words.

Additional Words

You'll find lists of **Additional Words** in each **Unit** in this Teacher's Guide.

These words give more examples of the sound/symbol just presented. These **Additional Words** include verbs and adjectives to supplement the nouns illustrated in each unit. Choose words from the list to add to students' vocabulary as appropriate. Demonstrate their meanings. You don't have to teach all of these words.

Providing the sounds

Choose an appropriate way to provide the sounds of the words:

1. The teacher, tutor, or English-speaking buddy can read the directions and tell the names of the pictured items. It's important that this be a person who speaks with excellent English pronunciation. This person should pace the aural input to the learner's ability and speed. You or others can use the **Audio Scripts** provided in this Teacher's Guide for each unit.

2. Audio CDs allow students to progress at their own pace. They are also essential if English is not your native language, and you can't provide a true example of standard American English pronunciation.

Each chapter of the Teacher's Guide lists the CD **Page and Track Numbers** that correspond to the pages.

3. Students who know the names of 90 percent of the pictured words won't need to depend on external audio input (CD, teacher, or tutor). However, occasional mistakes may occur when the student guesses the wrong name of an illustrated item (*kids* for *children*, *woman* for *mom*, for example).

Using the Audio CDs

The recorded units vary in length from 11 minutes to 28 minutes. The recording will read the instructions on each page. Then it will read new words three times. There is silence between repetitions so the student can say the words and feel the position of tongue, teeth, and lips as they make the sound and write the letters.

On challenge pages students will hear the words twice on the CD.

If the pace is too fast for a student, encourage him or her to review the unit "until it slows down."

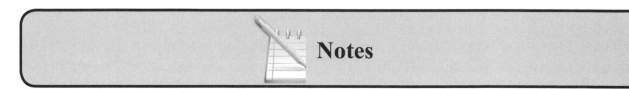

ESL Phonics for All Ages
Teacher's Guide
Book One:
Beginning Consonants

Overview

ESL Phonics Book One directs students' focus to the beginning sounds of words and the consonants that are used to spell those sounds. Students will encounter many pictures for many words they already know in English or will be learning in ESL class. The instructions will be simple. The presentation will allow for low anxiety, and the challenge will allow for success.

If you are teaching a group of students who are all at the same level in terms of phonics needs, you can use this Teacher's Guide as a language instruction handbook. There are suggestions for group presentations, classroom activities, conversations, and chanting and singing.

However, if your students are working on their own with the Audio CDs, there is no need to do that.

Each unit in **Book One** presents two beginning consonants and their sounds. The consonants chosen to be contrasted are very dissimilar in appearance, in sound, and in the written form to make the distinctions easier for the student.

Eight common words are given as examples

for each beginning consonant. Students learn sound/symbol correspondences at the same time they are developing vocabulary and listening skills. Following the presentation of the two dissimilar consonants, students are challenged to listen and recall the appropriate letters to write at the beginning of words. Following those pages, the student sees the words in simple, useful sentences, with the addition of common sight words. The sentences are presented in patterns to begin awareness of English sentence structure.

Each unit contains a conversation, song, or chant for memorization followed by sight reading.

Pages that are marked with a circled check mark at the bottom in the **Student Book** are challenge pages. These are pages that the student can self-correct, using the **Answer Pages**.

You'll find the **Track Numbers** and corresponding **Student Book** pages for each unit of **Book One** listed at the beginning of each unit.

The **Answer Pages** for **all books** are after page 91.

Book One, Unit 1: Student Book Pages 2-9

Contents of Unit 1

Page 1: Go over this list of icons with your students to make sure they understand the meaning of each symbol.

Challenge Pages

Page 4: This page introduces additional words with **b_** and **t_**. The student listens to each word and writes the beginning letter of the word.

Page 5: The student circles words that are the same. For example, if a given word is *teacher*, the student selects *teacher* from four other **t_** words.

Page 8: After students have learned the sentence pattern in this unit (*I have a tooth.*), they must match each sentence with the picture that illustrates the sentence. This page reviews the sentence pattern, and uses other words in the pattern. Students listen to and read the entire sentence.

Page 9: This **Read and Draw** activity only occurs in **Book One**. The students are given a sentence (using a pattern they have already practiced), and are challenged to draw a picture illustrating that sentence. The drawing verifies that the students have understood and illustrated the sentence correctly. Some teens and adults resist drawing. If this is the case with your students, skip this activity.

Song Suggestions

Page 6: This variation of the Happy Birthday song provides practice with the /b/ sound and also contrasts it with the /p/ sound in *happy*. Present the song via the CD to learn the variant melody created for us. Use the picture to build vocabulary: *birthday, baby, mother, father, grandmother, table, chair, cake, candle*, etc.

Sentence Pattern

Page 7: The sentence pattern illustrated in this unit is *I have a book.* This [Subject + Verb + Object] pattern is typical of those taught early in beginning ESL classes.

To enhance students' comprehension or mastery of the sentence pattern, conduct an oral lesson using small objects or classroom items. Have students practice with the item(s) in their hand or on their desk saying, *I have a book, I have a pencil,* etc. If it is appropriate for your students, you can introduce plural nouns in this pattern, since they do occur in this unit, as well. For example, *I have ten toes.*

Additional Words

The following list includes additional nouns, plus high-frequency verbs and adjectives that begin with **b** or **t**.

b_

back, bad, baloney, bank, baseball, beautiful, because, beach, bear, bedroom, beet, before, begin, berry, best, between, bite, bike, Bill, board, boat, bone, boo, boring, boss, bottle, bowl, brother, bug, build, burn, busy, butter, bye-bye

t_

tag, take, tall, tan, tap, tape, taste, teach, team, tell, tennis, test, terrible, tie, tight, tip, tiny, time, tired, to, today, together, tomorrow, tools, town, two, Tuesday, turkey, turn

 Notes

Book One, Unit 2: Student Book Pages 10-17

Contents of Unit 2

Challenge Pages

Page 12: This page introduces new words beginning with s_ and n_. The student is asked to write the beginning letter of each word.

Page 13: This page presents words beginning with s_ or n_. The student focuses on the whole word and circles the words that are the same.

Page 16: Students draw pictures illustrating sentences using words beginning with s_ or n_ in the sentence pattern, *I have a sandwich.*

Page 17: Students write the beginning letter of words using **s, n, b,** or **t.** The words are cued with pictures and students can also hear them on the CD. This activity reviews the **b_** and **t_** words from Unit 1 and the **s_** and **n_** words from this unit.

Sentence Pattern

Page 14: The sentence pattern here is the polite request with *may* and *please* as in *May I have a sandwich, please?*

Note that many speakers of American English will use the word *can* instead of *may*. We used to use *can* for ability and *may* for permission, but those distinctions are becoming blurred, as part of language change. We suggest teaching *may* for polite requests, but if some of your adult students bring up the fact that they hear people using *can,* you may just want to acknowledge this. Point out that the word *please* should be in a polite request.

Using classroom objects, demonstrate the use of polite requests with students. For example, *May I have (the book), please?* Then have students ask similar polite requests of each other. Teach students to say *thank you* and *you're welcome* in their responses.

Using page 14 in the **Student Book**, point to the picture of the girl and her thoughts about food. Elicit the names of the things she is asking for. Model the sentences as students read after you. Then ask students to read aloud individually or take turns with a partner. Do the same with the picture of the boy asking for other objects. Note that you can introduce the word *some* for mass nouns *(some soup, some salad)* or plurals *(some nickels)*.

Chant Suggestions

Page 15: This activity provides for rote learning of an enjoyable children's game and chant. The chant is based on the hand-slapping game, *Pease Porridge Hot.* Since *pease* and *porridge* are not useful words, we have substituted the more common words, *tuna sandwich.*

After you have demonstrated and taught the chant using the illustrations on page 15, do a hand clapping/slapping game with your students. There are various ways to do this. Here is one example:

Tuna sandwich hot,

Tuna:	(Slap your hands on your lap.)
sandwich:	(Clap your hands in front of you.)
hot:	(Slap your partner's hands.)

Tuna sandwich cold.

Tuna:	(Slap your hands on your lap.)
sandwich:	(Clap your hands in front of you.)
cold:	(Slap your partner's hands.)

My tuna sandwich

My:	(Slap your hands on your lap.)
tuna:	(Clap your hands in front of you.)
sandwich:	(Slap your right hand against partner's right hand.)

Is ten days old!

Is:	(Clap your hands.)
ten:	(Slap your left hand against partner's left hand.)
days:	(Clap your hands.)
old:	(Slap your hands against both of partner's hands.)

Have students practice the motions with a partner, repeating the sentences as you say them. Later, encourage students to take turns reading the chant from the blackboard as they practice until they can say it from memory.

You can also substitute other forms of food in this chant. For example, *egg sandwich, ham sandwich, rice and beans, cheese and tacos, huckleberries,* or whatever your students like to eat that has the right meter.

Additional Words

s_

safe, sand, same, Saturday, say, save, school, see, sell, September, seven, sick, silly, sister, sixty, size, soda, soldier, somebody, something, son, sour, subtract, summer, Sunday

n_

nap, nasty, navy, near, neat, need, neighbor, never, new, next, nice, no, nothing, nobody, November, now, nowhere, nut

Book One, Unit 3: Student Book Pages 18-27

Contents of Unit 3

Challenge Pages

Page 20: This page introduces additional words beginning with **j_** or **r_**. The student is asked to identify the beginning letter of each word.

Page 21: The student circles words that are the same. This page reviews **j_** words and **r_** words. The focus is on the whole word.

Page 24: Students draw pictures illustrating sentences using words beginning with **j_** or **r_** in the sentence pattern, *This is my jacket.*

Page 25: Students write the beginning letters of words using **b**, **t**, **n**, **s**, **j**, or **r**. This reviews and reinforces words previously used with these initial letters. Pictures also help cue the meanings of the words.

Page 26: Students write the beginning letters of words using **b**, **t**, **n**, **s**, **j**, or **r**, but there are no picture cues here. However, they can hear the words pronounced on the CD. If you do not have the CD, the **Audio Script** below lists the words you can dictate to the student as he or she writes the first letter of each word.

Words for Page 26*

1. bananas	2. seven	3. jar
4. ten	5. toes	6. nickel
7. radio	8. sun	9. book
10. neck	11. ruler	12. nest
13. jug	14. ball	15. teeth
16. rock	17. tiger	18. jet
19. bicycle	20. tea	21. nose

*Also on CD 1A track 26

Page 27: Students draw a line to connect the words that are the same.

Song Suggestions

1. The song *Jingle Bells* is known internationally and many of your students will already know it. Make sure they are pronouncing the letter **j** correctly. Also the word *sleigh* would be difficult to pronounce if students saw the spelling before being familiar with the word. They are being introduced to the discomfort that some English words are spelled in odd ways.

2. Divide the class into two groups. Have one group sing the regular lyrics while the other group just sings *jingle bells, jingle bells* repeatedly at the same time. Both groups should end together.

Sentence Pattern

Page 23: The sentence pattern in this unit is *This is my jacket*. This pattern [*BE* + Possessive Adjective + Noun] is used to indicate possession. Have students take turns holding up something of their own, and telling their classmates about it. For example, *This is my ring, This is my pencil*.

Additional Words

Have students use some of these words in the sentence pattern they have learned in this unit, as well as in the sentence patterns they already know. For example, *This is my jeep, This is my room, I have a rag, May I have some jelly, please?*

j_

January, jaw, jeep, jelly, job, jog, joy, July, jump, June

r_

rag, raw, reach, read, really, red, remain, remember, rent, report, rich, ride, right, ring, robin, room, rotten, round

 Notes

Book One, Unit 4: Student Book Pages 28-33

Contents of Unit 4

Challenge Pages

Page 30: This page reviews some words beginning with **p_** or **c_** and introduces new words with these beginning consonants. The student is asked to identify the beginning letter of each word.

Page 32: This page presents words beginning with **p_** or **c_**. The student focuses on the whole word and circles the words that are the same.

Page 33: After students have learned the sentence pattern in this unit (*She has a cat.*), they are now challenged to match each sentence with the picture illustrating that sentence. Students read the entire sentence, not just a word.

Sentence Pattern

Page 31: The sentence pattern illustrated in this unit is *She has a cat* [Subject + Verb + Object].

Have students sit in a circle, if appropriate. Each student holds up an object. One student starts and describes what he or she has. That same student then says what his or her neighbor has. For example:

Student A: *I have a notebook.*
He has a ruler.
Student B: *I have a ruler.*
She has a pen.

Additional Words

p_

pack, page, panda, papa, paper, party, pass, paste, peanut, peas, peel, people, pepper, perfect, pet, pick, picnic, pilot, pink, place, pocket, poem, police, pony, popcorn, potato, princess, print, prize, punch, punish, purple

c_

cake, call, camera, car, cash, cashier, cassette, clothes, coach, coffee, cold, color, comb, come, cone, cook, cop, copy, corner, cost, cough, country, cousin, cover, cowboy, cry, cucumber, cut

Book One, Unit 5: Student Book Pages 34-39

Contents of Unit 5

Challenge Pages

Page 36: This page introduces new words with **f_** and **d_**.

Page 38: After students have learned the sentence patterns in this unit (*What do you have? We have a football.*), they are now challenged to match each sentence with a picture.

Sentence Patterns

Page 37: In this unit, there are two sentence patterns; *What do (you) have? We have (a football.)*

Have students work in groups of three. One student asks the other two, *What do you have*? The other two then hold up something they are sharing and answer,

using the pattern. For example, *We have a ruler.* The students regroup and then a different student asks the question of the other two. And so forth.

Song Suggestions

The song, *Bingo,* is a well-known children's song. Present this song with the CD, or sing it. In susequent verses, another letter is missing; students clap instead of saying the letter.

Additional Words

Have students use some of these words in the sentence patterns learned in this unit, as well as in the sentence patterns they already know. For example, *What do you have? We have a diamond, I have a daughter, She has a friend.*

f_

factory, fail, fall, family, famous, far, fast, fat, favorite, feast, February, feel, fifteen, fill, find, finish, fire, first, fix, fly, fog, food, for, forgot, fountain, fourteen, free, freeze, Friday, friend, from, fruit, fry, funny

d_

Dan, dance, dangerous, daughter, day, dead, dear, Debbie, December, deep, denist, diamond, different, dig, discover, do, doctor, down, draw

Book One, Unit 6: Student Book Pages 40-45

Contents of Unit 6

Challenge Pages

Page 42: This page introduces new words with l_ or m_.

Page 44: After students have learned the sentence patterns in this unit *(What do they have? They have a mouse and a lion.)*, they are challenged to match each declarative sentence with a picture illustrating that sentence. Students read the entire sentence.

Page 45: Students draw pictures illustrating words beginning with m_ or l_ in the sentence pattern, *They have money and a map.*

Sentence Pattern

Page 43: In this unit, there are two sentence patterns. *What do they have? They have a mouse and a lion.* This pattern is [Subject + Verb + Object].

Give a pair of students various objects and have them come to the front of the room. Have other students ask questions and answer the questions using the patterns *What do they have?* and *They have a book and a pencil.*

Additional Words

Have students use some of these words in the sentences learned in this unit, as well as in the sentence patterns they already know. For example, *What do they have? They have a marble and a letter.*

m_

machine, mad, magic, main, make, manager, many, marble, March, mark, market, marry, May, maybe, me, medicine, meet, mess, mile, million, mistake, mix, Monday, month, morning, most, mother, move, movie, multiply, music, mustard, my

l_

lady, lake, large, Larry, late, laugh, laundry, lazy, learn, letters, light, list, listen, little, long, look, Lopez, Lorraine, Lucy

Book One, Unit 7: Student Book Pages 46-54

Contents of Unit 7

Challenge Pages

Page 48: This page reviews words beginning with **v_** or **z_** and introduces new words with these beginning consonants. The student has to write the beginning letter of each word.

Page 51: Students are challenged to write the correct beginning letter of various words presented in sentences using the pattern, *The pig is eating vegetables*. The

student has an opportunity to read and listen to the entire sentence, not just the isolated word. The beginning letters on this page are **p_, v_, l_, m_, d_,** and **f_**.

Page 53: Students draw pictures illustrating sentences using words beginning with **d_, f_, m_, p_, v_, b_, l_,** or **z_** in the pattern, *A dog is eating a fish.*

Page 54: Students write the beginning letters of words using **p_, c_, d_, f_, l_, m_, v_,** or **z_**, after hearing you say the words, or listening to the CD. The list below are the words you can dictate to the student as he or she writes the first letter of each word.

Words for Page 54

1. pencil	2. finger	3. map
4. vegetables	5. mouth	6. cat
7. pig	8. van	9. money
10. foot	11. duck	12. zero
13. zipper	14. door	15. picture
16. volcano	17. fish	18. car
19. football	20. mouse	21. doll

Poem Suggestions

The poem *Roses are Red* is a simple rhyming pattern that almost all American children and adults know by heart. It is a Valentine's Day message to express liking for another person.

When students can say the poem from memory, have them make up their own poems of four lines with the same rhyming scheme. Tell them they can use any words as long as they leave the word *blue* in line two and *you* in line four. Have students work in groups or pairs and then read their poems aloud to the class. Encourage fantasy and creativity. Here is an example:

> *The grass is green,*
> *The sky is blue,*
> *I'm from the U.S.,*
> *And so are you.*

Sentence Patterns

Pages 50, **51**, **53**: The man is eating lunch: [Subject + *BE* + Verb + *_ing* + Object]. Note that in some of the sentences on these pages, the object is a singular noun *(The monkey is eating a pie)*. In other sentences using this pattern, the object is either a plural noun (*vegetables*) or a non-countable noun (*lunch*).

Page 52: *Take the violets from the valley, Put the violets in the vase.* These are imperative forms. The pattern is [Verb + Object + Prepositional Phrase].

You can demonstrate the verbs *take* and *put* using actions with objects or pictures in front of you. For example, ask students to *Take a pen; Put the pen on the desk. Take a book; Put the book on the floor. Take a tissue; Put the tissue in your pocket.*

Have students work in pairs, with a set of simple objects in front of them on their desks (keys, penny, picture, paper, eraser, book, etc.) Practice giving commands to each other (in pairs or groups) using the pattern here, as other students follow the actions of the commands.

Additional Words

There aren't many common words in English that begin with the letters **v_** or **z_** .

v_

valentine, very, vet, visit, vocabulary, voice, vote

z_

zap, Zen, zither, zoo

Book One, Unit 8: Student Book Pages 55-61

Contents of Unit 8

Song Suggestions

Page 56: Present the song on the CD or sing it to them several times, acting out the motions of rowing. Say the words of each line several times and have the students say the words after you. Use gestures or pictures to explain words such as *row*, *boat*, *stream*, *gently*, *merrily*, *dream*.

After students have practiced the song, divide the class into two groups. Group 1 begins the song. When they have reach the word *stream* Group 2 begins the song from the beginning. When Group 1 finishes the song, they are to start again from the beginning. Each group sings the song three times.

With the song well-memorized, turn to the book and have students read the words. The memory of the words acts as clues to difficult words such as *gently, stream, merrily, dream.*

Challenge Pages

Page 59: This page introduces additional words with the hard sound of the letter **g_** and the letter **h_**. The student is asked to identify the beginning letter of each word. Spanish-speaking students who are literate in Spanish may have interference, as the letter *g* before *i* and *e* is prounounced similar to our *h*, and the letter *h* in Spanish is silent.

Page 61: This page presents words beginning with **g_** or **h_**. Words using the two different sounds of the letter **g_** occur on this page. The student focuses on the whole word and circles the words that are the same.

Chant Suggestions

This chant provides rhythmic practice with greetings *(Hi, Hello, How are you? I'm fine, thank you, How are you?)* and the sound of initial *h_*.

Hello and *good-bye* are slightly more formal than *hi* and *so long*. The word *thank you* is more formal than *thanks*.

After students have learned the chant by heart, divide the class into two groups, A and B.

Note that when Group A asks the question *How are you?*, the sentence stress is on the word *are*. When the question is asked the second time, (as Group B does), the stress is on the word *you*.

After the students have learned the chant, have them read the conversation in the book, allowing memorized words to clue their reading.

Elicit other expressions the students may have heard. For example, *Hey, What's up? 'Sup?* for *Hello* and *Bye, See you,* and *See you later.*

Additional Words

g_ (as in *girl*)

garden, Gary, get, ghost, give, go, gold, good, goose, governor, gown, grade, grandfather, grandmother, grasshopper, great, green, grow, guard, guess, guide, guy

g_ (as in *just*)

gel, gem, gender, gene, general, generous, genius, gentle, genuine, German, gesture

h_

handle, happy, hard, Harry, has, hate, he, help, her, here, hero, hide, high, highway, him, hit, hiccup, hiss, hole, home, how, hug, hum, hundred, hurry, hurt, husband

Notes

Book One, Unit 9: Student Book Pages 62-67

Contents of Unit 9

The letter **c_** has two different sounds at the beginning of words: the /k/ sound as in *cat* was presented in Unit 4. The letter **c_** has the /s/ sound when it comes before the letters **e**, **i**, and **y**. Page 62 of this unit presents **c_** words with the /s/ sound.

Challenge Pages

Page 64: This page presents words beginning with **w_** or **c_**. The student listens to the words (or remembers the name of the picture) and writes the beginning letter of each word. Both sounds of the letter **c_** appear on this page *(car, city)*.

Page 65: The picture on this page illustrates various words beginning with **w_** and the two different sounds of the beginning letter **c_**.

Have students look at the picture. Read the questions to them. Teach the words *can, see, yes,* and *no*. Demonstrate that they are to circle the words *Yes* or *No* on the page. For more suggestions on expanding this page, see the **Sentence Pattern** notes on the next page.

Page 66: Students write the beginning letters of words using **c_** , **g_** , **h_** , or **w_**, but there are no picture cues here. However, the student can hear the words pronounced on the CD. If you do not have the CD, the **Audio Script** below lists the words you can dictate to the student as he or she writes the first letter of each word.

Words for Page 66

1. cat	2. woman	3. horse
4. giant	5. hill	6. cup
7. heart	8. gym	9. water
10. giant	11. watch	12. house
13. circle	14. cow	15. card
16. calendar	17. cent	18. giraffe
19. city	20. window	21. hair

Page 67: Students are challenged to write the correct beginning letter of various words presented in illustrated sentences using the pattern, *The girl is looking at a game.* The student listens to the entire sentence. The beginning letters on this page are **c_** , **g_** , **h_** , and **w_**.

Sentence Pattern

Page 65: Question form using the modal auxiliary verb *can* for ability (rather than for permission or a request). The pattern is [(*Can*) + Subject + Main Verb + Object?] as in *Can you see a woman?*

In addition, the short answer forms *Yes, I can* or *No, I cannot/No, I can't* could be taught here, too. Note that the word *can't* is more conversational than *cannot*.

Before presenting the question pattern, play a modified game of *I Spy* and call it *I Can See*. Say a sentence about something you can see in the classroom and demonstrate that students are to point to the object you name. For example, *I can see a window, I can see a door.* If you want action in the classroom, have the students go to the object as you say it.

After students have learned the statement form, teach the question and answer forms. For example, *Can you see a door? Can you see a window? Yes, I can,* or *No, I cannot,* or *No, I can't.*

Additional Words

This section lists high-frequency verbs and adjectives, as well as additional nouns with the initial consonant sounds presented in this unit.

c_ (as in cat)

call, camera, carry, cash, cashier, cassette, coach, cold, color, comb, come, cook, cop, copy, corner, cost, cough, country, cousin, cover, cowboy, cry, cut, cute

c_ (as in city)

celebrate, cell, Celsius, cement, centigrade, central, century, cereal, certain, circus, citizen, cyber, cycle

w_

walk, wall, want, war, warm, wave, we, Wednesday, where, why, win, wind, wish, wonderful, worker, world

Book One, Unit 10: Student Book Pages 68-71

Contents of Unit 10

Challenge Page

Page 70: This page re-uses words beginning with **k_** or **y_** and introduces new words with these beginning sounds. The student has to write the beginning letter of each word. The words are cued with pictures.

Sentence Pattern

Page 71: *They are playing with a kitten.* This pattern is [Subject (plural) + BE + Verb + ING + Prepositional Phrase].

After students have practiced with the sentences on this page, hand out various objects, such as a book, pencil, ruler, ball, etc. Have some students, in pairs, pick one object and play with it together. Ask various other individual students to describe the action of the different pairs. For example, *They are playing with a ball, They are playing with a car*.

Additional Words

This section lists common useful verbs and adjectives, as well as additional nouns with that begin with **k_** and **y_**.

k_

Kate, kazoo, keep, keyboard, kick, kid, kimono, kind, king

y_

yard, year, yellow, yen, yes, yesterday, yogurt, young

Book One, Unit 11: Student Book Pages 72-79

Contents of Unit 11

This unit presents beginning digraphs (two consonants used together to represent one sound.) The beginning digraphs in this unit are **ch_**, **th_**, and **qu_**.

Note that the beginning letters **th_** can have two different sounds in English; the voiceless **th_** as in *thumb* and *thief*, or the voiced **th_** as in *this, these*, and *they*. In this unit, the words for **th_** all have the voiceless sound with the exception of the word, *these*.

Page 72, item 2, *children*: Point out that the *children*, means more than one *child*.

Page 76, item 4, *quart*: Make sure that students understand the illustration as a *quart* container and not *milk*. Explain that

a *quart* can be used for any liquid measure. For students more familiar with the metric system, you may have to explain that a *quart container* holds .95 liters.

Challenge Pages

Page 74: This page reviews words beginning with **th_** or **ch_**.

Page 78: This page reviews words beginning with **th_**, **ch_**, or **qu_**, and asks students to discriminate among the three beginning consonant clusters.

Page 79: Students write the beginning letters of words using **th_**, **ch_**, or **qu_**. (There are no pictures cues here.) They listen as you say the words, or as they hear the words spoken on the CD.

Words for Page 79

1. children	2. queen	3. thirty
4. quart	5. chair	6. cheek
7. thousand	8. cherries	9. thumb
10. chicken	11. quarter	12. quilt
13. quiz	14. thief	15. thirteen
16. check	17. question	18. thermometer

Chant Suggestions

Page 75: This chant practices the sounds of the beginning letters **th_** and **ch_**. It also provides practice with the polite expressions *thank you* and *you're welcome.*

After students have practiced the chant orally, write it on the board or on large chart paper and ask students to count the number of times they see the words *thank you, for,* and *the.*

Sentence Pattern

Page 77: *He is drawing a chair.* [Subject (pronoun) + *BE* + Verb + *_ing* + Object].

After students have practiced with the sentences on this page, have them work in pairs or in groups. Each student draws a picture of something. Their partners or group mates describe what that student is drawing. *What is [Paulo] drawing?* For example, *He is drawing a dog; She is drawing a cat.* Encourage students to use new vocabulary and some of the **Additional Words** (see next column) in this activity.

Additional Words

This section lists common verbs and adjectives, as well as additional nouns that begin with **th_**, **ch_** and **qu_**. Encourage students to use the words with the sentence pattern they have practiced in this unit, as well as with those they already know. For example, *He is drawing a child, She is drawing a chin, Thank you for the chocolate, They are playing with checkers.*

th_

thank you, theater, thermos, thick, think, third, thread, three, Thursday

ch_

chain, champion, change, chant, charge, Charles, chase, cheap, checker, chick, child, chin, chip, chocolate, choose, chop

qu_

quack, quartet, quartz, question, quick, quiet

 Notes

Book One, Unit 12: Student Book Pages 80-85

Contents of Unit 12

Challenge Pages

Page 82: This page reviews words beginning with **sh_** or **wh_**. The student is asked to identify the two beginning letters of each word. The words are cued with pictures.

Page 84: Students read the *Wh_* questions and answers previously practiced on page 83 and write the correct answers here. There is no audio.

Sentence Patterns

Page 83: Where's the whale?
[WH + BE + object.]
There it is. [There + pronoun IT + BE.]
It's number _____.
[IT + BE + predicate noun.]

Note the two possible answers on this page are *There it is* or *It's number _____*. Note the use of the contracted form of *where's* [where + is] and *it's* [it + is]. This is more conversational usage than using the full forms.

Song Suggestions

Page 85: This is a version of the well-known children's song, *Oh Where, Oh Where Has My Little Dog Gone?* The song provides practice with the *Wh_* question, beginning letters **wh_** and **sh_** and introduces additional words for **g_**, **h_**, **w_**, **c_**, **l_**, as well as reviewing **my**, **dog**, **little**, **tail**.

After students have memorized the song, divide the class into two groups and have them sing the song as a round.

Additional Words

This section lists common verbs and adjectives, as well as additional nouns beginning with sh_ and wh_.

sh_

   shake, shape, share, shave, she, shine, shop, shore, short, shout, shove, show, shower, shut, shy

wh_

   whack, what, when, whether, whisper, white, why

Book One, Mastery Tests: Student Book Pages 86-89

Contents of Mastery Tests

Page

86* Contrast:
   b_, t_, s_, n_, c_, r_, p_, j_
87* Contrast:
   f_, d_, m_, l_, v_, z_, g_
88* Contrast:
   h_, c_, w_, k_, y_, v_, s_
89* Contrast: **ch_, th_, qu_, sh_, wh_**
   * *Challenge Pages*

About Mastery Tests

The **Mastery Tests** on **pages 86** through **89** review beginning consonants and vocabulary. Students look at a picture and write the missing letter (or letters) at the beginning of each word. This challenges students' memory of the vocabulary as well as the letter that the words begin with. There is no audio for the **Mastery Tests.**

As a placement test: These **Tests** can serve as a placement test before a student begins to work alone on an individualized program. A score of 90% or better would indicate that a student has successfully completed **Book One**, or could skip **Book One**. A score of less than 70% indicates that it would benefit the student to start with **Book One**. Scores between 70% and 90% require your judgment based on the student's confidence, age, and the student's wishes.

Using the Mastery Tests

When students complete the **Mastery Tests**, you can notice which letters have given them problems. Have student review those sound/symbol correspondences referring back to the units that presented them.

Page 86: Students write the correct beginning letters for each of the eight words on this page. The beginning letters tested on this page are **b_, t_, s_, n_, c_, r_, p_**, and **j_**. Note that the letter **c_** as in *car* has the /k/ sound. Students who had trouble with this page can review Units 1-4.

Page 87: The beginning letters tested on this page are **f_, d_, m_, l_, v_, z_,** and **g_**. This page tests recall of the two different sounds for the letter **g_** as in the words *gym* and *girl*. Students who have trouble with these beginning letters, can review Units 5-8.

Page 88: The beginning letters tested on this page are **h_, c_, w_, k_, y_, v_,** and **s_**. This page tests the recall of the two different sounds of the letter **c_** as in the words *circle* with an /s/ sound and *calendar* with a /k/ sound. If students have trouble with any of these beginning letters, review Units 8-10.

Page 89: The beginning digraphs tested on this page are **ch_, th_, qu_, sh_,** and **wh_**.

Book One, Answer Pages

The **Answer Pages** for **All Books** start after page 91.

When a student has completed **Challenge Pages**, supply the answer page that corresponds to his or her work.

(Tear off the **Answer Pages** at the perforations. Keep them in a three-ring binder so you can photocopy them as needed.)

Demonstrate how the student is to mark his or her answers: C for correct, and X for an error.

Show the student the "My Work" page on page 92 in the **Student Book**. This gives a page number. The student counts the number of correct answers and writes it on the line.

Thus a student who got 8 right out of 8 on page 4 would write the number 8/8.

It reads "Page 4, eight right out of eight questions."

After a student has been self-correcting and self-tracking, you should check the progress on the **My Work** pages. If the tracking page shows that the student is getting everything right, give a lot of praise.

Check at random to see the pages that the student has corrected and verify that it is being done correctly. Ask the student to point to the pictures as you say the words, and later, to state the word for the picture.

The student needs to know that his or her progress means something to the teacher, and he or she has not been abandoned.

ESL Phonics for All Ages
Teacher's Guide
Book Two:
Ending Consonants

Overview

ESL Phonics Book Two directs students' focus to the ending sounds of words and the consonants that are used to spell those sounds. Students will encounter many of the same words that were presented in **Book One**. The instructions will be familiar as most are the same as instructions in **Book One**.

If the student is skipping **Book One**, then be sure he or she understands the meanings of the icons on page one.

Students who are working on their own with audio CDs may not need most of the various teacher instructions included. If you are teaching a group of students together and want to have more of an ESL-type lesson with them, these tips will be helpful.

Each unit in **Book Two** presents two to four ending consonants and their sounds. Eight common words are given as examples for each ending consonant. Students learn sound/symbol correspondences at the same time they are developing vocabulary and listening skills. Challenge pages ask students to listen and recall the appropriate letters at the ends of words. Following those pages, the student sees the words in simple, useful sentences.

Each unit contains a conversation, song, or chant for memorization followed by sight reading.

Pages that are marked with a circled check mark at the bottom in the **Student Book** are challenge pages. These are pages that the student can self-correct, using the **Answer Pages**.

You'll find the **Track Numbers** for each unit of **Book Two** at the beginning of each unit. The **Answer Pages** for **All Books** are after page 91.

Book Two, Review: Student Book Pages 1-3

Contents of Review Unit

Page		CD 2A Track
1	Icon recognition	1
2*	Review beginning consonants	2
3*	Review beginning digraphs	3
	Challenge Pages	

Page 1, Let's Begin: If students have completed **Book One**, review the meanings of the icons on page one. If you have determined that the student does not need **Book One**, then demonstrate the meanings and words for each icon. These are used in the headings and directions throughout **Book Two**.

Page 2, Review—Beginning Sounds: You can use this page either as a review if students have completed **Book One**, or as a diagnostic test if you feel they may be able to skip **Book One**. If students get 90% or more correct, they are ready for **Book Two**. If they get less than that correct, they should review sounds and letters from appropriate pages in **Book One**.

You can read the words to the student (see Words for Page 2/3) or the student can listen to the **Audio CD**.

The student should write the beginning consonants **b_, c_, l_, m_, h_, n_, t_, p_, d_, j_, y_, n_,** or **f_** at the beginning of the words.

There are no picture cues. Dictate the words in the boxes to the student.

Words for Page 2:

1. book 2. cook 3. look
4. mat 5. hat 6. bat
7. ten 8. hen 9. men
10. big 11. pig 12. dig
13. ham 14. jam 15. yam
16. jet 17. net 18. pet
19. man 20. can 21. fan

Page 3, Review—Beginning Sounds:

This page reviews beginning digraphs (**qu_**, **th_**, **sh_**, **wh_**, and **ch_**). The student should write the first two letters of each word as they hear them on the audio CD, or as you read them from the list below.

Words for Page 3:

1. queen 2. quarter 3. thousand
4. shirt 5. sheep 6. whale
7. where 8. thirty 9. quiz
10. chicken 11. shoe 12. question
13. think 14. quart 15. thank you

If you feel that students may already be competent with ending sounds, give the tests on pages 80 through 89 as a diagnostic test. Have students write their answers on a different sheet of paper, in case they are not going to be using the book. There is no point in marking it up in that case.

Book Two, Unit 1: Student Book Pages 4-11

Contents of Unit 1

This unit introduces and practices the ending sound /s/ so essential to both plural forms and third person singular forms.

Teach the word and the concept *end*. You can use words previously learned such as *foot, pen, leg, bus, sock, nose, rain, jam, carrot, pencil*. Write the words on the board and say all the letters. *What is the beginning letter? What is the beginning sound?*

Point to the end of the word *foot*. Say *foot*, exaggerating the /t/ sound. *What sound is at the end of this word? What sound is at the end of* pen? *What sound is at the end of* leg? *What sound is at the end of the word* foot? Repeat until students get the concept *ending sound*, and can distinguish it from *beginning sound*.

This unit may be confusing to students whose native languages do not have a plural forms for nouns (such as Japanese, Chinese, and Korean students).

Page 4, **More Than One:** Introduce the concept of one and more than one (singular and plural) nouns with objects the students can hold in their hands, such as *pen / pens; pencil / pencils; key / keys; book / books; cup / cups,* and so forth.

Have students practice asking and answering the question, *How many (pens) do you have? I have (two) (pens)*. (This question and answer are the two **Sentence Patterns** in this unit.)

Write the singular words on the board in one column labeled *One*. Write the corresponding plural words in another column labeled *More Than One*. Point to the *More Than One* column and ask, *What is the letter at the end of each word?* Point to the _s.

Say words from either column at random, and have students hold up one finger for *one*, and two fingers for *more than one*.

Have students read and repeat the words after you. Point out the ending sounds of the plural form again. Then do the same thing with the pictures and words on page 4.

Notes for Challenge Pages

Page 5: Students listen to the words on the CD to hear the ending sounds. If there is one item in the picture, they draw a circle around the word without an _s. If the picture shows more than one item, they circle the word with the _s. Note that all the plurals on this page end with the sound /s/.

Page 6: The same procedure. All the plurals on this page end with the sound /s/.

Page 7: All the plurals on this page end with the sound /z/.

Page 8: There are no picture cues here. Students must listen and distinguish the ending sound and circle either the singular or the plural form of the words they hear.

Say the word twice, giving students time to circle the correct word.

Words for Page 8:

1. bananas
2. toy
3. locks
4. pot
5. wheel
6. chairs
7. shoes
8. tiger
9. duck
10. bags
11. chickens
12. boot
13. radios
14. balloon

Sentence Patterns

Page 9: *How many cats do you have? I have three cats.*

Draw pictures of one cat, three dogs, four birds, two fish. Teach the vocabulary. Use two hand puppets go through the conversation several times, as you point to the pets. Ask students if they have any pets.

Encourage them to share that information using the sentence pattern, *I have (two) (pets).* Also teach the pattern *I don't have any pets.* Introduce pet vocabulary as needed: *hamsters, guinea pigs, snakes, lizards, parrots, crickets,* etc.

Song Suggestions

Page 10: This is a version of the well-known children's song, *Ten Little Indians.* The song reinforces numbers, plural nouns, and the enunciation of final /s/ or /z/.

Introduce the song with the CD or sing it to the students and have them learn it orally before seeing the words of the song in the book. Use your fingers to demonstrate the numbers. Emphasize the /z/ sound at the end of *readers.*

After the students have learned the song orally, introduce the written version. Read the words and have the students read after you. Have students find the word *happy* and tell how many times it appears (ten on each page). Have students count the numbers of readers they can find in the picture on page 10.

On page 10, the numeral is above each number word to give students a clue to the sound of the number word. On page 11, the numeral is in the far right column.

Students can create their own counting songs to practice more plural forms. Words of two syllables work best, such as *children, monkeys, chickens, teachers.* Students may change the adjective from *happy* to a different two-syllable adjective such as *little, silly, helpful.* They will need to come up with the additional adjective to replace the word *English.* Examples: *Mexican, Chinese, Japanese, Dominican, Brazilian, Arabic, Israeli, Egyptian...*and so forth.

Book Two, Unit 2: Student Book Pages 12-21

Contents of Unit 2

Challenge Pages

Page 14, page 18: Students listen to you or to the Audio CD or are cued by the pictures. They write the ending letter of each word.

Environmental Print

The term "Environmental Print" refers to words that students see around them on the street, on doors, in rest rooms, etc. Many of these words are crucial for students to learn for their own health and safety. Newcomers can't afford to wait until they know the phonics to sound out all these words. Learning them by sight will save confusion, embarrassment, and danger. The words on pages 15 and 21 help students to deal with environmental print they may encounter.

Page 15, *Bathroom Words*: Read the words to your students as you point to the pictures. Elicit or teach other terms for *bathroom*, such as *rest room, men's room, ladies' room* (or *women's room*), *washroom, lavatory,* or *toilet.*

If appropriate, ask male and female students to take a trip to the *men's room* or *ladies' room* and report back on the signs they find there.

Have students copy the signs they see. Write their words on the board and read them with the entire class. Make meanings comprehensible through gestures and pictures.

Page 21, *Street Signs*: The environmental print here consists of common signs found in the street. Read these words to the students.

Read the numbers and the words. Have students read the words after you. Have students find the same word in the picture. They should write the number in the circle next to each picture of the specific item. For example, students read *1. gas* in the list above the picture. Then they look at the picture, find the big sign with the word *Gas,* and write the number *1* in the circle to the left of the sign. Explain that the *G* is a big, or capital *g*.

Take a walk with students on a street near your school. Have them read the various signs they encounter, or you read the signs to them. Then have students copy the words they see on signs for homework. Invite students to share their words. Write their words on the board and read them with the entire class. Help make meanings comprehensible through gestures and pictures.

Chant Suggestions

Page 19: This chant is used with a "magic trick." The trick can provide motivation to memorize and read, as well as practice with the endings _ck and _ll.

Demonstrate the magic trick before presenting the written form.

Cut two very small squares about the size of your fingernails from black construction paper. Glue one square on one index finger, (the pointer) and the other on the other index finger. If you don't have the materials, blacken the fingernails of your index fingers with a *washable* black marker.

Sit at a desk or table with you on one side of the desk, and the students all on the opposite side.

Say the chant, and use the following motions:

Two little blackbirds sitting on a hill.

(Curl your other fingers into a fist and hide them under the table. Tap the edge of the top of the table with your two black-marked index fingers, one tap for each word or for each syllable.)

One named Jack,

(Tap with only your right index finger. Leave the other index finger on the table. Keep the other left hand fingers tightly curled into a fist, out of sight, under the table)

And one named Jill.

(Tap with only your left index finger. Leave the right index finger on edge of the table.)

Fly away, Jack!

(Quickly lift your right hand up in the air, over your shoulder and out of sight. When it is out of sight, quickly curl the marked index finger in with the others in your fist, and bring the unmarked middle finger down on the table to tap. This gives the illusion that the blackbird on the right hand has flown away. Students are not likely to notice that you have changed fingers. Keep the rest of your fingers in your fist under the table.)

Fly away, Jill!

(Do the same movement with your left hand and bring your left middle finger down on the table to tap, keeping the rest of your fingers in your fist under the table.)

Reverse the process to bring back the black birds.

Repeat the chant now that both black-marked fingers are tapping on the table again. Students are usually mystified. Do the trick several times; some students will catch on to what you are doing. If there are some students who can't understand how this trick is being done, do it very slowly and obviously.

Once the students have discovered the "magic," give each student two little black squares to glue to their index fingers. Give them an opportunity to say the chant and do the trick by themselves.

Sentence Patterns

Page 20: *When will you come back?*

The pattern, *I'll come back tomorrow* answers the *Wh_* Question with *will,* but it also uses the contracted form of *I + will.* Note that we can use the contracted form, *I'll* in the beginning of a sentence, but when *will* is the last word of a sentence, we use the full form, *Yes, I will.* The same is true for *Yes, he will* and *Yes, she will* in the conversation on this page.

Use puppets or draw two faces on the board and point to them as you act out the conversation. Demonstrate the word *tomorrow* by teaching the word *today,* pointing to the calendar at today's day. Then point to the next day and say *tomorrow.*

Have students repeat the text as you say it until they know it by heart. Have the students take turns asking the questions and saying the answers. Ask students questions about when they will come back or what they will do tomorrow. Present the written form on page 20. Read it with the students. Have individuals read it with help if necessary.

Additional Words

_n

tan, bacon, been, tin, win, Ben, den, begin, ton, win, John, born, brain, drain, burn, cabin, chin, clown, down, fun, heaven, hen, horn, Japan, lawn, learn, mean, moon, noon, ocean, onion, open, oven, ran, run, soon, then, tin, turn, van

_l

awful, boil, camel, canal, coal, equal, feel, final, fool, mail, meal, pupil, real, school

_ck

black, block, click, dock, kick, knock, lick, luck, pack, pick, quack, quick, shock, sick, snack, stuck, track, trick

_ll

all, Bill, bull, call, drill, fall, fill, full, hall, ill, mall, pill, pull, roll, spell, spill, still, tell, toll, yell

Book Two, Unit 3: Student Book Pages 22-27

Contents of Unit 3

Words for Page 25:

1. sun
2. cap
3. cat
4. can
5. school
6. pet
7. pool
8. lion
9. pot
10. stop
11. street
12. queen
13. ten
14. jacket
15. map
16. chicken
17. cup
18. foot
19. night
20. soap

This unit presents **_p** and **_t** as ending consonants. It reviews ending consonants **_n** and **_l** from Unit 2.

Challenge Pages

Page 24: This page presents words ending with **_p** or **_t**. The student writes the letter **p** or **t** at the end of each word.

Page 25: This page reviews the ending letters **_n** and **_l** from Unit 2 and reviews the ending letters **_p** and **_t**.

Read the words from the Word List below, or have students listen to the Audio CD. They then write the correct ending letters for the words here (**_n**, **_l**, **_p**, or **_t**).

Sentence Patterns

Page 26: The sentence patterns presented here are:
Is that your coat?
No, it's not my coat, it's Dan's coat.
Yes, it is.

The possessive adjectives *my* and *your* are presented here, as well as the possessive [apostrophe + **s**] with proper nouns.

Present the conversation with two hand puppets speaking the part. Have a coat to point to.

Have students practice the four conversations orally. Have students borrow an item from another student and ask pairs of students various questions and answers using the patterns on this page. For example, *Is that your (pencil)?, No, it's not my (pencil), It's Miguel's (pencil).*

Then have the students look at the page and read after you. Then have them read the conversation in pairs. Student A reads the question. Student B answers the question. Then reverse.

Point out to students that the [apostrophe + **s**] is used to show that something belongs to someone (*Jack's jacket*). Make sure the students understand that the [apostrophe + **s**] means a possessive or a contracted form and it doesn't make a word plural.

Song Suggestions

Page 27: This classic children's song uses rhythm and music to practice with words ending in **_t**.

Bring in a teapot and point to its parts; *handle, top,* and *spout.* Demonstrate the meanings of *short* and *stout.*

Speak the song and point to the parts of the teapot as you say them.

Listen to the song on the Audio CD.

Then sing the song and act out the song as below:

Have students practice the song and gestures, following your model. Once the students have learned the gestures, introduce the written form on a board or chart.

I'm a little teapot,
(Point to yourself.)

Short and stout.
(Gesture short by putting your hands palm down, low in front of you, then holding your hands out, palms in, to indicate round and fat.)

Here is my handle,
(Stand with your right hand on your hip with your elbow out to the right. This is the handle.)

Here is my spout.
(Hold your left upper arm close to your left side, with the forearm bent, pointing out towards your left.)

When I get all steamed up,
(Bounce up on your toes several times.)

Then I shout:
(Raise your voice a bit.)

"Tip me over and
(Bend to the left where the "spout" is.)

Pour me out!"
(Bend farther, as if tea is pouring out of the spout.)

You may want to teach the new sight words *(I'm, here, when, up, then).* You may also want to, if necessary, teach the fact that *I'm* is a contraction of [*I + am*].

Additional Words

This section lists high-frequency verbs and adjectives and additional nouns with the ending sounds presented in this unit.

_p

cheap, chop, clap, deep, dip, drip, group, help, hoop, hop, lap, nap, pop, scoop, sharp, shop, slap, soup, step, sweep, tap, tip, tulip, whip, zip

_t

art, at, bet, but, dirt, east, eat, exit, fast, fat, goat, got, heat, hit, hot, most, neat, next, pet, quiet, quit, rest, sat, shut, vest, went, west, wet, what

Book Two, Unit 4: Student Book Pages 28-37

Contents of Unit 4

This unit presents ending consonants _m and _r. It reviews ending consonants _p, _t, _ n, _l, _ck, and _ll.

Challenge Pages

Page 30: This page presents words ending with _m or _r. The student has to write in the ending letter of each word.

Page 31: This page reviews the ending letters _p and _t and contrasts them with _m and _r. The student writes the correct ending letter of each word.

Pages 33 and 34: These pages review the ending letters _l, _n, _m, and _r. On **page 34**, the student writes the correct ending letters for the words here, but there are no picture cues. Either dictate the words from the audio script below to the students or let them listen on the Audio CD.

Words for Page 34:

1. school	2. sun	3. star
4. mom	5. tail	6. pen
7. pool	8. lion	9. drum
10. water	11. mail	12. queen
13. ten	14. car	15. man
16. chicken	17. team	18. room
19. door	20. four	

Page 35: The student finds a word that is the same as the first word in a row.

Sentence Patterns

Page 32: *Wh_* Question, *Where are you from?* There are two varieties of answer: *I am from...* and *I'm from ...* Have students ask each other the questions and give their answers.

Use a world map to locate Japan, Mexico, and Canada, as well as the places your students are from. Model the question and answer; *Where are you from? I'm from (the U.S.).* On the board, write *I'm = I am.*

Page 36 presents a *Wh_* Question with *How many* or *How much,* and the verb *want.* (*How many bananas do you want?, How much money do you want?*) The answer includes number words, food words, money words, and the polite expression, *please. Here you are* and *Thank you* are in the conversation as well.

After students can say both parts of the conversation, have them read the text on page 36 after you. Have students take the part of customer and salesclerk and act out the conversation.

This page uses *How much* with money, which gives an opportunity to teach the words, values, and real items for *quarters, dimes,* and *nickels,* in addition to *dollars* and *cents.*

Song Suggestions

Page 37: *The Muffin Man.* If appropriate, bring in mini-muffins for the students to enjoy. Listen to the song on the CD or sing the song to the students. Have students practice with the *Yes/No* Question; *Do you know the muffin man*? and the answer; *Yes, I know the muffin man.* Teach *No, I don't know the muffin man.*

Expand to *Do you know the ESL teacher? Do you know the school nurse? The principal? The president of the United States?* Once students have learned the song, divide the class into two groups. Have Group 1 sing the question. Have Group 2 respond by singing the answer.

Additional Words

This section lists high-frequency verbs and adjectives, as well as additional nouns with the ending sounds presented in this unit.

_m

bloom, boom, cream, dream, from, gym, ham, hem, him, hum, prom, room, Sam, slam, storm, swim, them, Tom, warm, yum

_r

appear, brother, deer, ever, hear, ladder, mother, near, owner, pear, rear, singer, sister, storyteller, waiter

 Notes

Book Two, Unit 5: Student Book Pages 38-46

Contents of Unit 5

Challenge Pages

Page 40: This page reviews words ending with _b or _g and introduces new words with those ending consonants. The student listens to the teacher or the Audio CD and writes the ending letter of each word.

Page 44: This page reviews words ending with _d or _f. The student writes the correct ending letter for each word.

Page 45: This page reviews words ending with _d, _f, _b, or _g. The student writes the correct ending letter of each word.

Page 46: The student looks at the first word in a row of words. Paying attention to the ending as well as beginning letters, the student circles the word in that row that is the same.

Sentence Patterns

Page 41: *What's in the bag?* This question uses the contraction *What's* for [*What + is*].

Other patterns: *Is it a puppy? Yes, it is,* or *No, it isn't.* The ending sounds practiced here are _t, _g, and _b.

The question and answer patterns on this page are a basic form of the game *Twenty Questions.* Have puppets act out the conversation. Then have students repeat it after you.

Play the game with your students. Show five objects such as a pen, a book, and small plastic animals. Teach or review the names of the items.

Ask students to close their eyes as you put one of the objects into a paper bag. Hide the other objects elsewhere. Ask students, *What's in the bag?* Have students ask the questions as you answer. For example, *Is it a pen?, No, it isn't, Is it a ruler?, No, it isn't, Is it a calculator?, Yes, it is.* When a student guesses the correct item, have him or her put something into the bag and have classmates ask the questions. The "it" student answers.

Then open the book and read the questions and answers with the students reading after you.

Have students work in pairs to practice the questions and answers. Write the names of additional objects you can use in this game and help students read them.

Additional Words

_b

Bob, cab, club, cub, fib, grab, job, rub, scrub, tab, verb

_g

bag, big, dig, egg, fog, gag, hog, hug, jog, log, mug, plug, rag, tag

_d

add, bad, bead, bird, card, cold, dead, did, feed, food, Fred, glad, had, head, hid, kid, mad, mud, old, said, sat, Ted

_f

beef, cliff, elf, loaf, proof, puff, self, shelf, sniff, stiff, stuff

 Notes

Book Two, Unit 6: Student Book Pages 47-52

Contents of Unit 6

This unit presents the ending consonants _x, _ng, and _ss. The final _x is pronounced as /ks/ in English.

Page 49, **item 5**, *mess:* If appropriate, explain that the entire illustration means *mess*, not necessarily a broken *glass* and a cracked *egg*.

Challenge Pages

Page 50: This page reviews words ending in _x, _ss, or _ng. The student listens to the Audio CD and is asked to write the ending letter of each word.

Sentence Patterns

Page 51: The sentence patterns in this

unit use the auxiliary verb *can* (indicating ability, rather than permission). The pattern is [*Can* + Subject + Main Verb + Object?], as in *Can you fix my fan?* Students get practice using *can* in the question and *can* or *can't* in the answer. For example, *Can you fix my boat?, Yes, I can fix your boat, Can you fix my fan?, No, sorry, I can't fix your fan.* Point out that *can't* is the same as *cannot.* Note that *cannot* is spelled as one word, not two.

Present the conversations on page 51 using hand puppets. Have students repeat the questions and then the answers after the puppets. Then have students work in pairs to take the role of repair person and customer.

After the students know the conversation orally, turn to page 51 and read the text as students read after you.

Divide the class into two groups, each reading the part of one of the characters. Then have students work in pairs. Have students draw pictures of broken objects and then role play asking a partner, *Can you fix my (_____)?* The partner can answer, *Yes, I can fix your (_____),* or *No, sorry, I can't fix your (_____). (car, watch, clock, cell phone, notebook, nail clipper, etc.)*

Song Suggestions

Page 52: The song, *It's Raining, It's Pouring* is a well-known children's classic. If you have been talking about the weather regularly, students will probably know the phrase, *It's raining*, aurally. If not, or if you live in a dry climate, draw a picture of a large cloud dropping rain, and a stick figure of a person carrying an umbrella, as you introduce the phrase, *It's raining*.

Listen to the song on the CD, or sing the song to the students. Act out the verbs, *pouring, snoring, bumped*, and *went to bed*.

Say the words of the song and have the students say or sing the words after you or sing along with the CD. Point out that *didn't* is the same as *did not*.

For additional practice with this song, divide the class in four groups. The groups each practice their parts and then sing their parts simultaneously. Groups 1, 2, and 3 repeat their lines while Group 4 sings their lines only once. All groups end together.

Group 1 sings: *It's raining, It's raining,*

Group 2 sings: *It's pouring, It's pouring,*

Group 3 sings: *The old man is snoring,*

Group 4 sings: *He bumped his head*

When he went to bed,

And he didn't get up

The next morning.

Additional Words

The words presented in the **Student Book** are almost all nouns. This section lists high-frequency verbs and adjectives, as well as additional nouns with the ending sounds presented in this unit. Encourage students to use these words with the sentence patterns they have practiced in this unit. For example, *Can you fix my swing?, Yes, I can fix your swing.* You may also use main verbs from the **Additional Words** below (other than *fix*) with the pattern practiced in this unit. For example, *Can you mix water and juice?, Can you relax on a swing?*

_x

lynx, mix, prefix, relax, suffix, tax, wax

_ng

anything, cling, ding, everything, fling, sling, spring, swing, thing

_ss

across, bless, boss, brass, guess, hiss, lass, less, miss, press

Book Two, Unit 7: Student Book Pages 53-63

Contents of Unit 7

This unit presents ending consonant digraphs _sh, _th, _ch, _tch, and _dge.

The letters _th in *mouth* and *math* are voiceless.

The ending letters _tch have the sound /ch/ as in *watch*.

The ending letters _dge have the sound /j/ as in *judge*.

Page 53, item 4, *rash*: You may have to demonstrate or explain the word *rash*.

Page 54, item 7, ¼: The fraction ¼ is *pronounced one fourth.*

Challenge Pages

Page 56: This page reviews words ending with _sh or _th. The student looks at the word cues or listens to the **Audio CD** and writes the ending letter for each word.

Page 57: This page reviews words ending with _th or _ch. The student writes the ending letters of each word.

Page 58: This page reviews words ending with _ch, _sh, or _th. The student now has to distinguish among three different ending sounds and write the correct ending letters for each word.

Page 59: This page reviews words ending with _ch, _sh, or _th. The student looks at a line with five words, and has to circle two matching words. There is no audio, and there are no picture cues in this activity.

Page 62: This page reviews words ending with _dge or _tch. The student looks at the pictures and listens to the **Audio CD** to decide which letters to write at the ends of the words.

Page 63: This page reviews all the ending sounds taught in this unit (_sh, _th, _ch, _tch, and _dge). The student is asked to focus on whole words and circle two matching words from a group of five words.

Additional Words

_sh

wish, wash, bash, cash, dash, hash, lash, mash, sash, mesh, gosh, josh, slosh, bush, push, crush, gush, hush, mush, rush, slush

_th

fifth, month, myth, sixth, moth, both, oath, Beth, Seth, Ruth, death, truth

_ch

coach, couch, each, much, ouch, pinch, porch, punch, ranch, reach, rich, such, teach, touch, which

_tch

match, watch, catch, latch, batch, patch, fetch, ditch, hitch, pitch, stitch, witch, Dutch, hutch

_dge

budge, fudge, grudge, sludge, nudge, wedge, fridge, ridge, dodge

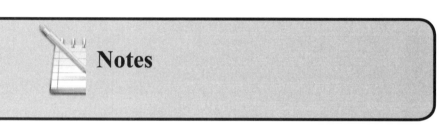

Notes

Unit 8: Student Book Pages 64-71

Contents of Unit 8

The Fox and the Goat

This unit presents an old Aesop's tale. Students listen to the story as they read the words. The pictures will help them understand the story. They are recognizing words already learned and new words. Students practice the beginning and ending consonants that have been learned in **Books One** and **Two**.

1. As students listen, have them point to the panel of the story that they hear, and track the sentences with their fingers. Present the new vocabulary in the story through gestures, actions, or pictures. Point to the pictures or act out the words such as: *well, fell, get out, thirsty, down, saw, up, down, good, drink, jump, Mmm, good, back, help, long time, leap.*

In a second reading, you can have the students repeat each sentence as you read.

Ask comprehension questions.

Page 64: Who fell into a deep well?
   Could the fox get out?

   Who came to the well next?

   Was the goat hungry or thirsty?

Page 65: What did the goat see in the well?

   What did he ask the fox?

   What did the fox say?

   What did the goat do?

Page 66: Was the water good or bad?

   What did the fox say?

   Was there a way to get out?

What did the fox say next?

Page 67: How did the fox get out of the well?

What did he do next?

Did he help the goat?

How did the goat get out of the well?

General Opinion Questions:

Did you like the fox?

Did you like the goat?

What did the goat learn?

Was the fox good to the goat?

Answers will vary. For example, answers might be, *Look before you leap, Always be careful, I didn't like the fox, I liked the goat.*

2. Within a page, say a sentence at random and have students tell you the number of the panel it is in.

3. Have students read aloud individually, with teacher assistance, if needed. Praise efforts and good work.

4. Have students work in pairs, alternating reading the panels of the story.

5. Prepare a sentence strip for each panel. Have various students each hold a strip and then physically organize themselves in the actual sequence of the story. Each student reads his or her sentence in correct sequence.

6. Photocopy the next page. Give each pair of students the pages, and have them cut the page into sentences. Write the first sentence on the board. Have students arrange the sentences on their desks to retell the story. Have students check their story with the sentences in the student book.

7. Have students take the parts of the characters and act out the story.

8. Have students retell the story in their own words.

9. The moral or underlying lesson of this story is, "*Look before you leap.*" Explain that *leap* is another word for *jump*. Ask students if they have a similar proverb in their home countries. Have them tell the group. Have them tell what other lessons they can learn from the story. (Don't believe a stranger. Get promises in writing...)

Note that the narrative part of the story is in the simple past tense while the conversations are in the present tense.

Challenge Pages

Pages 68, **69:** These pages present multiple choice statements to review the sentence structures and vocabulary and to verify the student's comprehension. Students draw a circle around the best word to complete each sentence.

Have students work in pairs or alone to complete the activity. Have them read their answers aloud.

Page 70: This page focuses who said what in various parts of the story—the fox or the goat. Point out the quotation marks and teach the phrase *quotation marks.* Say, *When you see these marks, it means someone is talking.*

Do the exercise orally. For example *Who said, "Is the water good?"* Have students tell you the answer (*The goat*). Then let students work on their own to read and answer the questions.

Page 71: This page tests understanding of the sequence of events in the story.

Teach the concepts and vocabulary for *first, next, then,* and *last.* Line students up at the door. Ask, *Who will go out the door first? Who is next? Who comes after him/her? Who is last?* Using a wall calendar, ask, *What is the first day of the week? What day is next? What day comes after that? What is the last day?*

Read the sentences aloud as they occur on the page (out of order).

Ask, *What happened first? (A fox fell into a well).* Point out the number "1" next to that sentence on the page. Ask, *What happened next? (The goat jumped into the well).* Have students write the number "2" in front of that sentence. Continue asking the question, *What happened next?* Have students write the appropriate number next to each sentence. Then have the students read the sentences in the correct order.

Notes

Book Two, Unit 9: Student Book Pages 72-76

Contents of Unit 9

About The Mice, the Cat, and the Bell

In Unit 9, students hear a story read to them as they follow along in the text, getting meaning from the illustrations. They encounter known vocabulary in context and learn new vocabulary.

Students will encounter words with beginning and ending consonants which they have practiced in Books One and Two. Many of the sentence patterns will also be familiar.

Read the story to the students or have them listen to the Audio CD. As students listen, have them point to the panel of the story that they hear, and track the sentences with their fingers. Point to the picture or act out the words such as: *afraid, mice, meeting, talked, hear, because, hooray, shout, kill, who, want, easy,* and *do.*

In a second reading, have the students repeat each sentence as you read.

Ask comprehension questions for each page:

Page 72:

> *Who liked to eat mice?*
> *Did the mice like to eat cats?*
> *Were the mice afraid of the big cat?*
> *Was the cat afraid of the little mice?*
> *Who had a meeting; cats or mice?*

Page 73:

> *What did one little mouse say?*
> *What can they put on the cat?*

Page 74:

> *How will a bell on the cat help the little mice?*
> *Did they put a bell on the cat? Why not?*

1. With students' attention on a particular page, say a sentence at random and have students tell you the number of the panel it is in.

2. Have students read aloud individually, with teacher assistance, if needed.

3. Have students work in pairs, alternating reading the panels of the story.

4. Have students take the parts of the characters and act out the story.

5. Have students retell the story in their own words.

6. The moral or underlying lesson of this story is, "*It's easier to say things than to do them*," or "*Talk is cheap*."

7. Ask students if they have a similar proverb in their home countries. Have them tell the group. Have them tell what other lessons they can learn from the story. (*Actions speak louder than words*.)

Note that the narrative part of the story is in the simple past tense while the conversations are in the present tense. Many of the sentence patterns have been previously practiced in Books One and Two.

Challenge Pages

Pages 75, 76: These pages present multiple-choice statements which test the student's comprehension of the story and ability to read. Students select the word that best completes the sentence. For example, *A big cat liked to eat _____.* Students choose the word *rice* or *mice* to complete the sentence.

First review the vocabulary with the pictures at the top of page 75. Read the first sentence with the blank. (*A big cat liked to eat _____.*) Say *blank* for the blank. Read the two choices (*rice, mice*). Have students tell you which word is correct. Have them circle the correct word and copy it on the line. Have students work in pairs or alone to complete the rest of the activity. Then have them read their answers aloud.

Book Two, Unit 10: Review and Mastery Tests Student Book Pages 77-89

About the Tests

The tests on pages 77 to 89 can be used in many ways. First, they can be used as diagnostic tests to see if students need the lessons in **Book Two**. If students score 85% or better, they can go on to **Book Three**.

If students have worked through **Book Two**, the tests can be used as a review before moving on to **Book Three**, or they can be used as an evaluative tool to judge the students' achievement.

Some students will enjoy the idea of a test, and will do well. Others may develop anxiety if it seems there are consequences for not doing well. Always allow a student to feel some success. Praise the success.

Use the CD or read the Audio Scripts below to dictate the words to the students. Say each word two times (or more, if necessary) and give students enough time to write the ending letter.

Words for Page 77: (One ending letter)

1. map	2. cat	3. bug
4. beg	5. dog	6. job
7. hoof	8. book	9. pool
10. arm	11. leg	12. cut
13. star	14. six	15. rat
16. bread	17. crab	18 big
19. girl	20. soup	21. gas

Words for Page 78: (Two ending letters)

1. math	2. fish	3. sing
4. wash	5. peach	6. grass
7. bath	8. lunch	9. fourth
10. dish	11. mouth	12. punch
13. back	14. king	15. cloth
16. class	17. brick	18 swing
19. check	20. kiss	21. truck

Words for Page 79: (Three ending letters)

1. match	2. hedge	3. badge
4. catch	5. crutch	6. pitch
7. stitch	8. judge	9. itch
10. bridge	11. ledge	12. smudge
13. pledge	14. watch	15. edge

The **Mastery Tests** on pages 80 through 89 are all labeled **"Read and Write."** These **Tests** review vocabulary learned in Books One and Two as well as both beginning and ending consonants

These **Mastery Tests** can demonstrate to the student, as well as to the teacher, the progress that has been made in Books One and Two. Oversee the correction of the **Tests** or allow students to self-correct, whichever is appropriate.

There is no audio in this unit. Students look at each picture and choose the word in the shaded box at the top of the page. Student writes the correct word under each picture.

These **Tests** can also serve as a placement test prior to beginning an individualized program. A score of 90% or better would indicate that a student could skip **Books One** and **Two** and progress to **Book Three** immediately. A score of less than 65% indicates that it would benefit the student to review **Book One** and/or **Book Two**. Use your own judgement for scores in between those two.

Notes

Book Two, Answer Pages

The **Answer Pages** for **All Books** start after page 91.

When a student has completed **Challenge Pages**, supply the answer page that corresponds to his or her work.

(Tear off the **Answer Pages** at the perforations. Keep them in a three-ring binder so you can photocopy them as needed.)

Demonstrate how the student is to mark his or her answers: C for correct, and X for an error.

Show the student the "My Work" page on page 92 in the **Student Book**. This gives a page number. The student counts the number of correct answers and writes it on the line.

Thus a student who got 8 right out of 8 on page 4 would write the number 8/8.

It reads "Page 4, eight right out of eight questions."

After a student has been self-correcting and self-tracking, you should check the progress on the **My Work** pages. If the tracking page shows that the student is getting everything right, give a lot of praise.

Check at random to see the pages that the student has corrected and verify that it is being done correctly. Ask the student to point to the pictures as you say the words, and later, to state the word for the picture.

The student needs to know that his or her progress means something to the teacher, and he or she has not been abandoned.

ESL Phonics for All Ages
Teacher's Guide
Book Three:
Consonant Clusters

Overview

Book Three helps the new reader tackle consonant clusters (two or three consonants together). New speakers of English may find it difficult to distinguish such sounds as they may not occur in their native language. There are fewer common words with these consonant clusters, so the examples may not be familiar to them aurally before encountering them here.

Each consonant cluster is presented with several examples. A second cluster is presented with examples, and, as in the previous books, the two clusters are contrasted.

Units One through **Five** present consonant clusters that occur in the beginning position in a word, as in *clock, frog,* and *star.*

Unit Six presents consonant clusters in final position as in *hand, ant, nest.*

Unit Seven presents final _le as in *apple, bottle* and *little.* All of the common consonant cluster endings are contrasted.

Unit Eight presents consonants in the middle of words: single consonants as in as *baby, woman,* and *potato;* digraphs as in *mother, teacher, washer,* and double consonants in the middle of words as in *rabbit, hammer, puzzle,* and *balloon.*

The letter *x* is treated as a consonant cluster, as it has two consonant sounds, /k/ and /s/.

Unit Nine is a story, incorporating the lessons learned in this and previous books.

See the **Series Overview** and the **Activity Types and Procedures** section on pages 5 to 23 in this **Teacher's Guide** for more strategies.

If your students are using the Audio CDs, they can progress at their own pace with minimal instruction needed from a teacher. Students can repeat a lesson as many times as needed. If you are not using the CDs, you'll find the words to dictate in these pages.

The **Track Numbers** for the Audio CDs for **Book Three** are listed for each unit. The **Answer Pages** for **All Books** begin after page 91.

You may photocopy the **Answer Pages** so students can easily check their own answers. Show students how to track their progress by adding their correct answers and entering that number on the correct line on page 92 in the **Student Book**.

Book Three, Unit 1: Student Book Pages 5-16

Contents of Unit 1

Pages 5, 6, 7: Presentation of beginning consonant clusters cl_, fl_, pl_. Student listens, says the word, and writes the two letters at the beginning of the word.

Pages 12, 13, 14: Presentation of bl_, gl_, sl_.

Challenge Pages

Page 8: Student listens to the word, says the word, and writes correct consonant cluster at the beginning of the word.

Page 9: The student is to find the words which are the same in each line and draw a circle around each of them.

Page 10: Student listens, looks at the pictures, and draws a circle around the correct sentence for each picture.

Page 15: Student listens, says the words, and writes the correct consonant clusters at the beginning of the words.

Page 16: Student looks at the five words in each row and draws a circle around the two words that are the same.

Sentence Patterns

Page 10: Sentence patterns practiced in this unit are:
Please pass the plate.
Please [verb + direct object].
Please clap for the clown.
Please [verb + prepositional phrase].

Song Suggestions

Play the song on the CD or on *Easy Songs for English Language Learners*. As you present the song, clap your hands as indicated below.

Have students join in the singing as they feel ready. Have them clap where indicated below, and twice after the words *Clap your hands!* For example:

If you're happy (clap) *and you know* (clap) *it,*
Clap your hands! (clap, clap)
If you're happy (clap) *and you know* (clap) *it,*
Clap your hands! (clap, clap)
If you're happy (clap) *and you know* (clap) *it,*

Then you really (clap) *ought to show* (clap) *it.*

If you're happy (clap) *and you know* (clap) *it,*

Clap your hands! (clap, clap)

Additional Words

Select the words that you feel are appropriate for the ages and levels of your students. If necessary, demonstrate the meaning of the words by actions, pictures, pointing, or using them in an example sentence.

cl_

clam, clarinet, clasp, class, classmate, claw, clay, clean, clear, clever, clerk, click, cliff, climate, climb, cling, clip, close, cloth, clover, club, clue, clumsy

fl_

flap, flash, flat, flavor, flea, flesh, flew, flier, flight, fling, float, flock, flop, fluffy, fluid, flush, flutter, flute, fly

pl_

place, plain, plan, planet, plaster, plastic, plate, play, please, pledge, plenty, plow, plug, plum, plunger

bl_

black, blame, blank, blanket, blaze, bleed, blend, bless, blew, blimp, blind, blink, blister, blob, block, blond, bloom, blow, blue, blush

gl_

glad, glance, glare, glaze, gleam, glee, glide, glimmer, glitch, gloat, glob, gloom, glory, gloss, glow

sl_

slam, slang, slant, slash, slate, slave, slay, sleek, sleet, sleigh, slice, slick, slight, slim, sling, slip, slit, sliver, slob, sloppy, slot, slow, slug, slurp

 Notes

Book Three, Unit 2: Student Book Pages 17-30

Contents of Unit 2

Challenge Pages

Page 20: On this page, students listen to the words and write **cr_**, **fr_**, or **pr_** at the beginning of each word.

Page 21: On this page students find two words in a row that are the same.

If students have trouble discriminating these sounds, make a list of on the board with two columns. Put all the words with consonant clusters with /l/ in Column One and those with /r/ in the Colume Two. Tell students to raise one finger when they hear a word from column one and two fingers when they hear a word from column two. Randomly say words from either column.

Pages 25, 26: These **Challenge Pages** review the next set of consonant clusters with /r/; namely **br_**, **dr_** , and **gr_**.

Pages 28, 29: These **Challenge Pages** review the consonant clusters taught in **Unit 2** and contrast them with those taught in **Unit 1**. **Page 29** contains full sentences with the sentence pattern [The (Noun) is (Verb) ing.]

Page 30: This **Challenge Page** reviews all of the clusters presented with audio input only. Students must listen attentively and just be cued aurally without picture cues. See the **Audio Script** below to dictate the words if the student is not using the **Audio CD**.

Words for Page 30

1. ground	2. prize	3. drink
4. friend	5. fry	6. cry
7. grandmother	8. crown	9. brush
10. brain	11. brown	12. green
13. crayons	14. frog	15. prince
16. drum	17. grass	18. fruit
19. drive	20. dress	21. brother

Sentence Patterns

Page 29: Two sentence patterns are practiced.
The frog is frozen.
[Subject + BE + adjective.]
He's crossing the road.
[Subject + *BE* + Verb + *_ing* + Object].

Song Suggestions

Page 27: Many of your students will be

familiar with the melody of this song (*Frère Jacques*). Teach the song for aural memorization first. Sing it yourself, or have students listen to it on the Audio CD or on *Easy Songs for English Language Learners*. Clarify the meanings of the new words. For fun, divide the class into two groups and have them sing the song as a round.

Additional Words

Have students use some of these words in the sentence patterns they have learned. For example, *The fries are free, My brother is brave.* Have students, in teams or pairs, say a word from one of the groups below while the other team or student identifies the consonant cluster. For example, Team A: *place*, Team B: **pl_**.

cr_

crack, cradle, craft, cramp, crane, crash, crate, crawl, creak, cream, crease, create, creature, credit, crew, crime, crisp, croak, crocodile, croon, crop, crowd, cruel, crumb, crunch, cry, crystal

fr_

fragrant, frail, frank, fraud, free, freedom, freeze, freight, frenzy, fresh, friction, fridge, fried, fries, fright, frigid, frizz, frog, from, front, frost, frown

pr_

practice, praise, prayer, preach, precious, predict, prefer, prefix, prepare, preschool, preserve, president, press, pressure, pretend, pretty, pride, primary, principal, print, problem, produce, professor, program, project, promise, protect

br_

braces, brake, brand, brave, breath, breeze, brew, bride, brief, bright, bring, broadcast, broccoli, broke, brother, brown, bruise, brunch, brunette, brush

dr_

draft, drag, drain, drama, drank, drawing, dried, drill, drink, drip, drizzle, drone, drool, droop, drop, drown, drumstick, dry

gr_

grab, grace, grade, grammar, grand, grant, grateful, grave, gravy, gray, grease, great, green, greet, grief, grin, grind, groom, grouch, ground, group, grow, grumpy, grunt

Notes

Book Three, Unit 3: Student Book Pages 31-42

it with the rest of the word. Examples: sssssssssssssstudent; sssssssssssstar; ssssssssssssssstove.

Challenge Pages

Pages 34, **38:** These **Challenge Pages** each review three consonant clusters. If students have trouble with any of these, review the individual sounds on the presentation pages. (See **Contents at a Glance** section to the left.)

Page 40, **Puzzle:** The task for students is to find the words in the word list hiding somewhere in the puzzle. Words may be written from left to right, and from up to down. This simplified Word Search is a fun way for students to review the consonant clusters in this unit and the two previous units.

Page 41, Listen, Find, and Circle:

Students have to find two words that are the same on a line, and draw a circle around those two.

Page 42: These pages review the consonant clusters taught in this unit. Read the words from the Audio Script, or have students listen to the words dictated on the CD. They have to listen carefully, and write the two letters at the beginning of each word.

The consonant clusters in this unit are combinations of the consonant **s** followed by **t**, **p**, **m**, **k**, **n**, and **w**. These clusters are often difficult for English language learners, especially for Spanish speakers. This type of cluster does not occur in initial position in Spanish. Students will tend to add a vowel before the initial cluster so that the word *student,* for example, becomes *estudent.*

Page 31, st_: Help Spanish speakers pronounce initial **s_** clusters. Have them hiss the /s/ sound and sustain it. Then follow

Words for Page 42

1. sleep	2. smile	3. sleeve
4. spot	5. spoon	6. star
7. stove	8. skeleton	9. skirt
10. smoke	11. sneeze	12. snake
13. snore	14. skin	15. sweep
16. smart	17. swim	18. snow
19. statue	20. stem	21. speak

Sentence Patterns

Page 39: The sentence patterns in this unit demonstrate the future tense with *will* (*They will swing*). Some of the sentences demonstrate the use of prepositional phrases with *will* (*They will stand on the steps; They will ski in the snow*). Have students take turns pantomiming the actions in these sentences. You can also practice the sentence patterns with the **Additional Words** listed below in this unit, if appropriate to your students.

Additional Words

Encourage students to use some of these words in the sentence patterns with *will* on page 39. For example, *They will starve, He will stand in the stadium.* Have students work in groups and help them to read their best sentences to the class.

st_

stab, stable, stack, stadium, staff, stag, stage, stain, stake, stale, stall, stampede, standard, staple, stare, start, starve, stash, state, static, station, statue, stay, steak, steal, steam, steel, steer, storm, story

sp_

space, span, Spanish, spare, spark, speak, spear, special, speck, speed, spell, spend, spoil, sponge, sport, spout, spur, spurt, spy

sm_

smack, small, smart, smash, smear, smirk, smog, smooth, smug, smuggle

sk_

skateboard, skeleton, skeptic, sketch, skid, skill, skillet, skim, skimp, skin, skip, skit

sn_

snag, snap, snarl, snazzy, sneak, sniff, snob, snoop, snooze, snorkel, snout, snug

sw_

swab, swallow, swam, swamp, swap, swarm, sway, swear, sweet, swell, swept, swift, swirl, swiss, swollen, swoop, swore

 Notes

Book Three, Unit 4: Student Book Pages 43-49

Contents of Unit 4

Many of the students will have trouble with the **thr_** initial consonant cluster, since this sound doesn't exist in many other languages. It is also difficult to pronounce the **th** immediately followed by the /r/ sound.

It can be useful to do discrimination practice with words beginning with **thr_** and words with initial /s/ or /t/ sound. For example, *thread, said; throw, so; three, tea.*

You may also do discrimination practice with **thr_** and **tr_**. Discrimination practice is a necessary step to pronunciation of the different phonemes. However, at this level the student needs only to know how to read words that begin with **thr_**, not pronounce them.

Challenge Pages

Page 47: This page reviews and contrasts all of the consonant clusters presented in this unit.

If students have trouble with this page, they should return to the presentation page for the appropriate consonant cluster.

Page 49: This page reviews the consonant clusters, but without illustrations. Students are cued by the words on the CD or the words you read to them. This page reviews not only **tr_**, **tw_**, and **sc_** from this unit, but it also reviews the consonant clusters **st_** and **sn_** previously taught in Unit 3. The students are challenged to discriminate among five consonant clusters.

Words for Page 49

1. twinkle	2. scarf	3. snake
4. train	5. twins	6. snack
7. school	8. truck	9. twelve
10. twenty	11. trash	12. trap
13. scale	14. snore	15. tracks
16. tweezers	17. star	18. scoop
19. tray	20. trophy	21. twig

Song Suggestions

Page 48: Many of your students will be familiar with the melody of this song *(Twinkle, Twinkle, Little Star)*. Review the words first. Then divide the class into three groups and have them sing the song as a round.

Another variation of this is to divide the class into two groups. One group sings or chants the regular lyrics and the other group chants, *Twinkle, twinkle, twinkle, twinkle,* simultaneously and repeatedly while the first group completes the regular lyrics. This rhythmic rendition reinforces the rhythm and intonation of the words and helps as a memory aid.

Additional Words

Select the words that you feel are appropriate for the ages and levels of your students. Recycle some of the sentence patterns used in Units 1 through 3 and use these words in those patterns, as appropriate. For example, *Please play the trumpet, Please pass the twine, He's writing the word twice, The trailer is red.*

tr_

trade, tradition, traffic, tragedy, trail, trailer, trait, translate, transparent, trap, trapeze, trash, travel, treasure, treat, trial, tribe, trick, trio, trip, trouble, true, trumpet, trust, try

tw_

tweak, tweed, tweet, twelfth, twice, twilight, twine, twirl, twist, twitch

thr_

threat, threw, thrifty, thrill, throat, throb, throne, through, threaten

sc_

scald, scallop, scan, scandal, scar, scare, scold, scooter, scope, scorn, scout, scowl, scuff

 Notes

Book Three, Unit 5: Student Book Pages 50-59

Contents of Unit 5

The consonant clusters in this unit consist of three letters that each make their own sound. These will be difficult for many students to distinguish aurally, so repeat practice may be needed to hear and distinguish the sounds. Don't focus on having students pronounce the sounds: that is a higher order of difficulty.

Page 53, squ_: squ_ is pronounced as /skw/.

Page 52, item 5, *spruce:* A *spruce* is a type of tree.

Page 53, item 6, *squat:* Demonstrating to your students that *squat* is different from *sit*.

Challenge Pages

Page 55: This page reviews and contrasts the consonant clusters **scr_**, **spl_**, **spr_**, **squ_**, **str_**. Students draw a circle around two words that are the same in a group of five words.

Page 56: This page contrasts the consonant clusters **scr_**, **spr_**, **squ_**, **str_**, and **thr_**.

Page 58: This page challenges the student to listen and discriminate among the consonant clusters **scr_**, **spr_**, **squ_**, **str_** and **thr_** without any illustrations to cue them. The **Audio Script** for this page appears below.

Words for Page 58

1. square	2. street
3. spring	4. throne
5. squirrel	6. strawberry
7. stripe	8. square
9. throw	10. scream
11. thread	12. spread
13. strong	14. stream
15. spring	16. three

Sentence Patterns

Page 57:
He will squeeze the strawberry.
He will splash in the street.
[He will + VERB + Object]

Chant Suggestions

This chant is well known to Americans. It shows a contrast between *I scream* and *ice cream*. The difference between these two phrases is that in the first phrase (*I scream*) the **scr_** links with *eam*. In the second phrase, the **s** links with the *I* before it; only the **cr_** links with *eam*.

Students can have fun with this in class. Say, *I scream* and *ice cream* for your students several times to give them practice in discriminating between them.

Additional Words

Select the words that you feel are appropriate for the ages and levels of your students. Have students try to use some of these words in the sentence patterns of this unit or of previous units. For example, *She will scramble the letters.*

scr_

  scram, scramble, scrape, scratch, screen, script, scroll

spl_

  splatter, splice, splurge

spr_

  sprain, spray, spread, spree, sprinkle, spry

squ_

  squad, squaw, squawk, squeak, squid, squish

str_

  strength, stress, stretch, stretcher, strict, strike, string, stroke, stroll, stroller, strong, structure, struggle

Notes

Book Three, Unit 6: Student Book Pages 60-69

Contents of Unit 6

The consonant clusters in this unit are "word-final" consonant clusters. These are challenging for many reasons. In many other languages, consonant clusters do not occur in word ending position.

Some speakers of American English don't always enunciate these final consonant clusters clearly. Often final consonants are reduced. For example, we sometimes hear words with the final **_nd** as in *around* pronounced without the final /d/ sound (*aroun*). A similar phenomenon occurs with **_st** as in *toast*, **_sk** as in *ask*, and with **_ft** as in *loft* and *draft.*

While we want to teach our students Standard American English pronunciation, they may be hearing a reduced form of these consonant clusters on the street, in the movies, and on TV.

You may also want to have students distinguish between words with the final consonant clusters and those with a single final consonant such as *tent / ten, plant / plan,* as well as *sink / sin, tank / tan, pink / pin.* This is actually different from the reduction phenomenon discussed above where the language is changing and the reduction of the cluster doesn't change the meaning of the word. For example, *toast* vs. the non-Standard English *toas.*

Page 67, item 8, *stump:* A stump is the part of a tree that remains after the tree has been cut down.

Challenge Pages

There are two **Challenge Pages** in this unit for **_st**, **_nt**, **_ft** contrasts and one for contrasting **_nk**, **_nd**, **_mp.** If students have difficulty with any of these pages, direct them to the presentation page for the appropriate consonant clusters.

Page 63: On this page, students are asked to discriminate among the **_st**, **_nt**, **_ft** final consonant clusters and write the appropriate letters at the ends of the words.

Page 64: Students discriminate among the words containing the final clusters **_st**, **_nt**, **_ft.** They draw a circle around two words that are the same in a group of five words.

Page 68: On this page, students are asked to discriminate among the **_nk**, **_nd**, **_mp** final consonant clusters and write the appropriate letters at the ends of the words.

Song Suggestions

Page 69: *The Bear Went Over the Mountain* is a traditional song in American culture. Present the song with the Audio CD or sing it to the class using pictures to get the meaning across. Coach the pronunciation of *mountain,* so students hear and can say the **nt** in the middle of the word.

Say each sentence of the song as the class says it after you. Play the CD again and let students sing along.

Divide the class into two groups. After all the students have practiced the words, have them respond to each other. Group One sings the first stanza. Group Two sings the second stanza (the question).

Group One responds with the answer.

Additional Words

Select the words that you feel are appropriate for the ages and levels of your students.

_st

best, east, fast, host, just, last, mast, mist, past, pest, rest, rust, west, beast, blast, boost, burst, coast, crust, feast, first, least, roast, roost, waist

_nt

aunt, bent, hint, hunt, mint, sent, vent, want, went, count, event, front, meant, mount, paint, saint, slant, spent, stunt

_ft

left, lift, soft, craft, theft

_nk

bunk, dunk, drank, Frank, yank, blink, plank, plunk, prank, rank, spank, thank, think, trunk

_nd

band, bend, bond, land, lend, mind, find, pond, tend, wind, blend, blind, brand, found, mound, pound, round, sound, spend, stand

_mp

camp, damp, dump, jump, lump, ramp, wimp, cramp, plump, stamp, swamp, thump

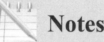

Notes

Book Three, Unit 7: Student Book Pages 70-75

Contents of Unit 7

The main sound in this unit is the **_le** in word-final position. This is pronounced as /əl/.

English language learners may tend to pronounce the **_le** so it sounds like the French word, *le*.

Note that almost this entire unit is devoted to words that end in **_le**, as opposed to the other units in **Book Three** which usually have one presentation page per sound.

Page 70, **item 2**, *icicle*: Note that the first **c** is pronounced as an /s/ sound, and the second **c** has a /k/ sound.

Page 70, **item 5**, *puzzle*: Note that the illustration for the word *puzzle* here shows a jigsaw puzzle. Students can also see the **Puzzle** on page 73.

Page 71, **item 3**, *dimple*: Point out that a dimple is a small recession in the skin, often on the cheek.

Page 72, **item 2**, *whistle*: Point out to students that the letter **t** is silent in the word *whistle*. In some dialects of American English **wh** is pronounced as /hw/, while in other dialects **wh** is pronounced as /w/ without the /h/ sound. Both are considered correct.

Challenge Pages

Page 73, **Puzzle:** All the words in this puzzle have the final written **_le**.

There is a list of words at the top of the page. Students have to search for these words and draw a ring around them in the puzzle. The words may be in horizontal rows, or in vertical columns.

Page 75: This **Challenge Page** reviews all of the final consonant clusters taught in **Unit 6** (**_st, _nt, _ft, _nk, _nd, _mp**), as well as the **_le** introduced in this unit. Students must listen carefully. They have only an aural sound to go by, and no picture cues.

Words for Page 75

1. bottle	2. point	3. sink
4. ghost	5. bubble	6. hand
7. plant	8. kettle	9. gift
10. apple	11. sand	12. stamp
13. trunk	14. draft	15. pump
16. ankle	17. toast	18. tent
19. tank	20. people	21. needle

Sentence Pattern

Page 74: The pattern is [*There* + *BE* + Object + Prepositional Phrase]. Note that *there is* is used with singular nouns (*There is a turtle*). You may also want to introduce the plural form of the verb *BE* in this same pattern for use with plural nouns (*There are two turtles on the table*).

Page 74, *in / on*: Students may need discrimination practice with *in* versus *on* in the prepositional phrases which are part of the sentence pattern on page 74. Since both *in* and *on* occur in an unstressed position in the sentence, it may be difficult for students to recognize the difference in pronunciation.

Also you may need to reinforce the difference in meaning between the prepositions *in* and *on*. Demonstrate this difference by using *in* and *on* in sentences with classroom objects. For example, *The pen is on the book. / The pen is in the book*. Act out each sentence while students say the appropriate sentence. Continue this with other classroom objects.

Additional Words

Select the words that you feel are appropriate for the ages and levels of your student.

_le

battle, beagle, beetle, buckle, bundle, cable, castle, couple, cuddle, doodle, eagle, fumble, gamble, gargle, gentle, google, handle, humble, hurdle, jiggle, jungle, maple, marble, meddle, mumble, nibble, noodle, peddle, pickle, raffle, rumble, simple, title, uncle, wiggle

 Notes

Book Three, Unit 8: Student Book Pages 76-83

Contents of Unit 8

This unit helps students to focus on consonant sounds in the middle of words.

Students have seen some of these words before.

Page 80, items **3**, **7**, **8**, *washer, catcher, teacher*: Many students will have challenges distinguishing between the /sh/ sound in *washer* and the /ch/ sound in *catcher* or *teacher*. This is especially true for Spanish speakers who don't have the /sh/ sound in their language. They will tend to substitute the /ch/ sound whether the /sh/ is in the initial, medial, or final position in the word.

Do a discrimination practice with the following words for your students: *catch / cash, latch / lash, batch / bash, hatch / hash*. Even though these two sounds are in final position, such discrimination practice will help students recognize their differences when they occur in the middle of a word.

Page 81, **item 6**, *middle*: You may need to clarify that the word being illustrated is *middle* and not *circle*. Note that the arrow is pointing to the middle circle.

Page 82, **item 4**, *coffee*: You may need to clarify that the word *coffee* refers to the hot liquid that is usually served in a cup or coffee pot, rather than the words *cup* or *coffee pot*.

Challenge Pages

In this unit, all of the pages are **Challenge Pages**.

Additional Words

Since the consonants in this unit are so varied, there are no additional words listed here. Have your students practice the words in this unit with sentence patterns used throughout **Student Book Three**.

Book Three, Unit 9: Student Book Pages 84-90

Contents of Unit 9

About the Story

This unit focuses on a story. Many of the words in the story use consonant clusters that have been practiced in **Book Three**.

Read the story to the students, using the pictures and actions to help with the meanings of *grasshopper, ants, ground, frozen, summer, winter, died, work, play, plenty of, nothing*. (Or have students listen to the story on the CD.)

See pages 21 and 22 in the **Overview** section for general suggestions for presenting a story. These include reading the story, having students listen to the CD, reviewing each panel of the story with its illustrations, explaining new vocabulary, and having the students read the story aloud.

After each page, ask comprehension questions:

Page 84:

What did the grasshopper love to do?

What did he eat all summer?

What were the ants doing?

Why did the ants do this?

What did the ants say to the grasshopper?

Page 85:

Did the grasshopper listen to the ants?

What happened in the winter?

What was frozen?

Who had plenty of food?

What did the grasshopper have to eat?

Page 86:

Who went to the ants' nest?

What did the grasshopper ask for?

Did the ants give the grasshopper anything?

Who played now?

Have students tell the story in their own words. Do they know this story in their own language? Does it end the same way? (In some cultures, artists and creative people are valued for their contributions. The story begins the same but the ants invite the grasshopper into their home in the winter so he can play music for them while they dance.)

The moral of this version of the story is "Work before you play." After the students have fully understood the story, ask them whether they have a similar saying in their home countries.

Note that the narrative part of the story is in the simple past tense and the quotes are in the present tense.

Challenge Pages

Pages 87, **88:** These pages present statements from the story with one word left out. Students have to choose the correct word from two possible choices.

Page 89: This page tests students on story comprehension by asking which character made each statement. Explain the purpose and meaning of quotation marks in conversation.

Page 90: This page focuses on the sequence of events in the story. The first event is labeled (__1__ *The grasshopper played all summer.*) Students have to write number 2 in front of the second thing that happened in the story, number 3 on the next and so forth.

Notes

Book Three, Unit 10: Student Book Pages 91-93

Contents of Unit 10

This unit consists of three **Review Tests**. The student will have to have aural input to know what to write (although some word endings may serve as clues, for example __ __ andmother cannot have any two letters other than **gr_**. On the other hand, there are various possibilities for __ __ ant, __ __ ake, and __eep, so students must pay attention to the aural input.)

Students listen to the words and then write the missing letters.

The Review Tests can also serve as a possible placement test. If students score less than 65%, they could benefit from working with or reviewing **Book Three** before proceeding to **Book Four**.

Oversee the correction of the **Review Tests** or allow the students to self-correct, whichever is appropriate for your students. The audio scripts appear below for each **Review Test**.

Page 91, **Review 1:** This page reviews the following beginning consonant clusters taught in **Book Three: cl_ , pl_ , fl_ , sl_ , bl_ , pr_ , br_ , fr_ , dr_ , st_ , cr_ , sm_ , sk_ , gr_ , tr_ , sn_ , sp_ , tw_ , sw_**.

Page 92, **Review 2:** This page reviews some of the three-letter clusters (trigraphs) taught in Unit 5. The beginning consonant clusters

reviewed here are: **scr_ , spl_ , str_ , squ_ , spr_**.

Page 93, **Review 3:** This page is a comprehensive review of the ending clusters taught in **Book Three**. These are: **_st, _nt, _ft, _le, _mp, _nk, _nd**.

Words for Page 91

1. closet	2. plant	3. flower
4. plane	5. sleep	6. blanket
7. prize	8. brush	9. friend
10. drive	11. star	12. crayons
13. smoke	14. skirt	15. grandmother
16. truck	17. snake	18. spaghetti
19. twenty	20. train	21. sweater

Words for Page 92

1. scrub	2. splash
3. string	4. strawberry
5. squirrel	6. square
7. street	8. sprinkle
9. stripe	10. squint

Words for Page 93

1. nest	2. plant	3. gift
4. apple	5. hump	6. junk
7. bottle	8. skunk	9. friend
10. toast	11. people	12. count
13. sink	14. noodle	15. left
16. drink	17. stamp	18. middle

Book Three Answer Pages

The **Answer Pages** for **All Books** start after this page.

When a student has completed **Challenge Pages**, supply the answer page that corresponds to his or her work.

(Tear off the **Answer Pages** at the perforations. Keep them in a three-ring binder so you can photocopy them as needed.)

Demonstrate how the student is to mark his or her answers: C for correct, and X for an error.

Show the student the "My Work" page on page 92 in the **Student Book**. This gives a page number. The student counts the number of correct answers and writes it on the line.

Thus a student who got 8 right out of 8 on page 4 would write the number 8/8.

It reads "Page 4, eight right out of eight questions."

After a student has been self-correcting and self-tracking, you should check the progress on the **My Work** pages. If the tracking page shows that the student is getting everything right, give a lot of praise.

Check at random to see the pages that the student has corrected and verify that it is being done correctly. Ask the student to point to the pictures as you say the words, and later, to state the word for the picture.

The student needs to know that his or her progress means something to the teacher, and he or she has not been abandoned.

Listen and Write

Listen to the words.

Say the words.

Do the words begin with the sound /b/ or /t/ ?

Write the letter **b** or **t** at the beginning of each word.

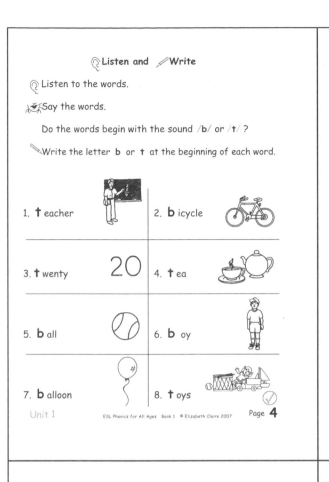

1. **t** eacher	2. **b** icycle
3. **t** wenty 20	4. **t** ea
5. **b** all	6. **b** oy
7. **b** alloon	8. **t** oys

Listen, Find, and Circle

Listen to the word.

Find a word that is the same.

Draw a circle around the same word.

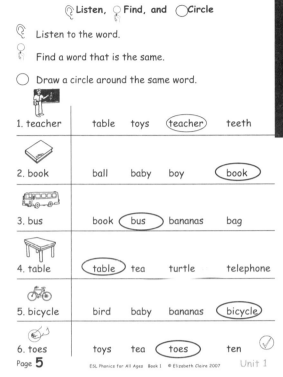

1. teacher	table	toys	(teacher)	teeth
2. book	ball	baby	boy	(book)
3. bus	book	(bus)	bananas	bag
4. table	(table)	tea	turtle	telephone
5. bicycle	bird	baby	bananas	(bicycle)
6. toes	toys	tea	(toes)	ten

Read and Find

1. (I have a tooth.)
2. (I have a book.)
3. (I have a turtle.)
4. (I have a baby.)
5. (I have a bird.)
6. (I have a telephone.)

Read and Draw

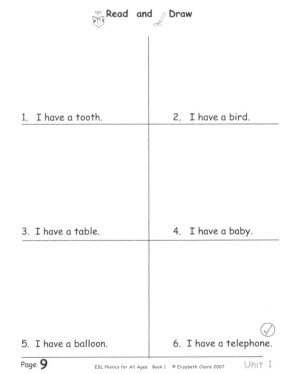

1. I have a tooth.	2. I have a bird.
3. I have a table.	4. I have a baby.
5. I have a balloon.	6. I have a telephone.

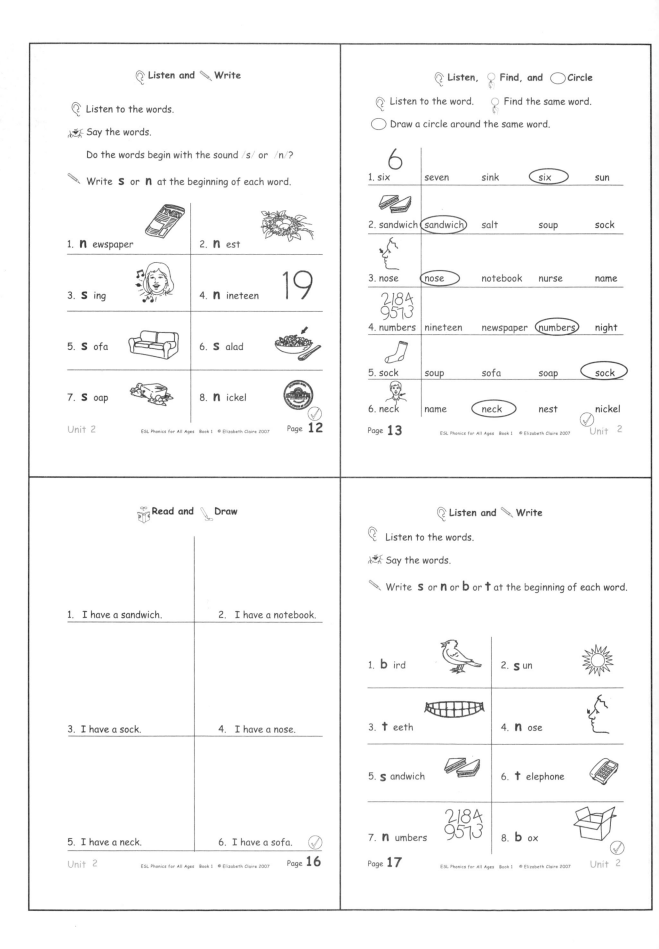

👂 Listen and ✏️ Write

👂 Listen to the words.

🗣️ Say the words.

Do the words begin with the sound /s/ or /n/?

✏️ Write **s** or **n** at the beginning of each word.

1. **n** ewspaper	2. **n** est
3. **s** ing	4. **n** ineteen
5. **s** ofa	6. **s** alad
7. **s** oap	8. **n** ickel

👂 Listen, 🔍 Find, and ⭕ Circle

👂 Listen to the word. 🔍 Find the same word.

⭕ Draw a circle around the same word.

1. six	seven	sink	(six)	sun
2. sandwich	(sandwich)	salt	soup	sock
3. nose	(nose)	notebook	nurse	name
4. numbers	nineteen	newspaper	(numbers)	night
5. sock	soup	sofa	soap	(sock)
6. neck	name	(neck)	nest	nickel

📦 Read and ✏️ Draw

1. I have a sandwich.	2. I have a notebook.
3. I have a sock.	4. I have a nose.
5. I have a neck.	6. I have a sofa.

👂 Listen and ✏️ Write

👂 Listen to the words.

🗣️ Say the words.

✏️ Write **s** or **n** or **b** or **t** at the beginning of each word.

1. **b** ird	2. **s** un
3. **t** eeth	4. **n** ose
5. **s** andwich	6. **t** elephone
7. **n** umbers	8. **b** ox

Listen and Write

Listen to the words.

Say the words.

Do the words begin with the sound /j/ or the /r/?

Write **j** or **r** at the beginning of each word.

1. **r** ake		2. **j** udge	
3. **r** adio		4. **j** ug	
5. **r** oad		6. **j** ack-o'-lantern	
7. **j** eans		8. **r** ing	✓

Listen, Find, and Circle

Listen to the word.   Find the same word.
Draw a circle around the same word.

 1. jam	jug	jail	jar	(jam)
 2. jet	(jet)	jacket	juice	jar
 3. jug	jar	(jug)	juice	jam
 4. rat	rug	rake	ring	(rat)
 5. rug	jug	(rug)	road	rake
 6. ruler	radio	jumper	(ruler)	rock	✓

Read and Draw

1. This is my rabbit.	2. This is my jack-o'-lantern.
3. This is my jacket.	4. This is my radio.
5. This is my jug.	6. This is my ring. ✓

Say and Write

Look at the pictures.   Say the words.

What's the beginning sound?

Write the beginning letter for each word.
b, t, n, s, j, or **r.**

1. **j** acket		?. **n** ine	9
3. **s** andwich		4. **t** eeth	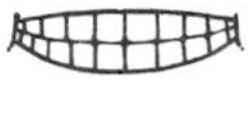
5. **b** ird		6. **n** eck	
7. **t** elephone		8. **b** ox	✓

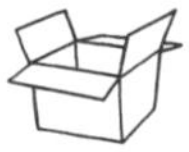

Book 1

Top-left panel

👂 Listen and ✎ Write

👂 Listen to each word.

What's the beginning sound?

✎ Write the letter **b**, **t**, **n**, **s**, **j**, or **r**.

1. **b** ananas	2. **s** even	3. **j** ar
4. **t** en	5. **t** oes	6. **n** ickel
7. **r** adio	8. **s** un	9. **b** ook
10. **n** eck	11. **r** uler	12. **n** est
13. **j** ug	14. **b** all	15. **t** eeth
16. **r** ock	17. **t** iger	18. **j** et
19. **b** icycle	20. **t** ea	21. **n** ose

Top-right panel

👁 Find the Same Word

👓 Look at the words.

✎ Draw a line to the words that are the same.

1. ring — rice
2. rice — road
3. road — ring
4. jet — jacket
5. jacket — jet
6. jam — rat
7. rat — ruler
8. ruler — jam

Bottom-left panel

👂 Listen and ✎ Write

👂 Listen to the words.

🗣 Say the words.

Do the words begin with the sound /p/ or /k/?

✎ Write **p** or **c** at the beginning of each word.

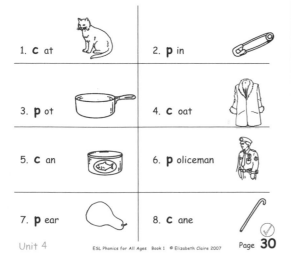

1. **c** at	2. **p** in
3. **p** ot	4. **c** oat
5. **c** an	6. **p** oliceman
7. **p** ear	8. **c** ane

Bottom-right panel

👂 Listen, 👁 Find, and ◯ Circle

👂 Listen to the word. 🎲 Read the word.
◯ Draw a circle around the same word.

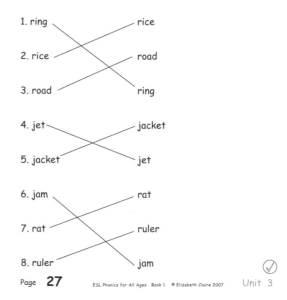

 1. pig	picture	pan	piano	(pig)
 2. picture	piano	pencil	(picture)	pie
 3. puzzle	pants	pear	(puzzle)	piano
 4. cat	cup	coat	(cat)	car
 5. carrot	cat	cup	(carrot)	car
 6. calendar	cat	cow	(calendar)	cane

Top left panel

🎲 Read and ◯ Find

1. She has a cat.

2. She has a puzzle.

3. She has a calendar.

4. He has a carrot.

5. He has a pig.

6. He has a picture.

Top right panel

👂 Listen and ✎ Write

👂 Listen to the words.

🗣 Say the words.

Do you hear the sound /f/ or the sound /d/?

✎ Write **f** or **d** at the beginning of each word.

1. **f** ootball		2. **f** ifty	50
3. **d** oor		4. **d** oll	
5. **f** ather		6. **d** ancer	
7. **f** eet		8. **d** irty	

Bottom left panel

🎲 Read and ◯ Find

What do you have?

1. We have a fish.

2. We have a dog.

3. We have a doll.

4. We have a dollar.

5. We have a football.

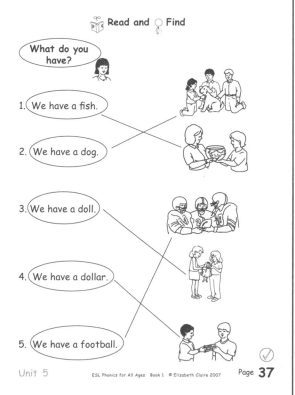

Bottom right panel

👂 Listen and ✎ Write

👂 Listen to the words.

🗣 Say the words.

Do the words begin with the sound /l/ or /m/?

✎ Write **l** or **m** at the beginning of each word.

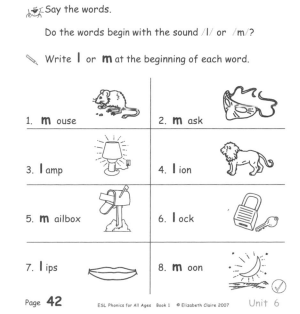

1. **m** ouse		2. **m** ask	
3. **l** amp		4. **l** ion	
5. **m** ailbox		6. **l** ock	
7. **l** ips		8. **m** oon	

Read and ⭘ Find

What do they have?

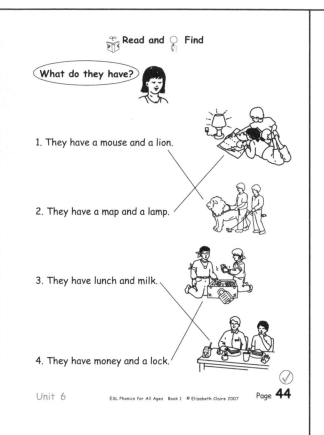

1. They have a mouse and a lion.

2. They have a map and a lamp.

3. They have lunch and milk.

4. They have money and a lock.

Read and ✏ Draw

1. They have milk.	2. They have money and a map.
3. They have a lamp and a lock.	4. They have a mouse.
5. They have lunch.	6. They have a lion.

Listen and ✏ Write

🔊 Listen to the words.

🗣 Say the words.

Do the words begin with the sound /v/ or /z/?

✏ Write **v** or **z** at the beginning of each word.

1. **v** iolet	2. **z** ipper
3. **v** acuum cleaner	4. **v** alley
5. **v** itamin	6. **z** ero
7. **v** iolin	8. **v** isitor

Listen and ✏ Write

🔊 Listen to the sentences.

What letters are missing?

✏ Write the beginning sounds.

1. The **p** ig is eating **v** egetables.

2. The **p** oliceman is eating a **l** emon.

3. The **m** an is eating **l** unch.

4. The **d** og is eating a **f** ish.

5. The **m** onkey is eating a **p** ie.

Read and Draw

1. A dog is eating a fish.	2. A man is eating a duck.
3. A pig is eating vegetables.	4. A boy is eating a lemon.
5. A zebra is eating a leaf.	6. A fish is eating a volleyball.

Listen and Write

Listen to each word.

What's the beginning sound?

Write **p**, **c**, **d**, **f**, **l**, **m**, **v** or **z**.

1. **p** encil	2. **f** inger	3. **m** ap
4. **v** egetables	5. **m** outh	6. **c** at
7. **p** ig	8. **v** an	9. **m** oney
10. **f** oot	11. **d** uck	12. **z** ero
13. **z** ipper	14. **d** oor	15. **p** icture
16. **v** olcano	17. **f** ish	18. **c** ar
19. **f** ootball	20. **m** ouse	21. **d** oll

Listen and Write

Listen to the words.

Say the words.

Do the words begin with the sound /g/, /j/, or /h/?

Write the letter **g** or **h** at the beginning of these words.

1. **g** ift	2. **g** as
3. **h** and	4. **g** arbage
5. **h** at	6. **h** eart
7. **g** ame	8. **h** ill

Listen, Find, and Circle

Listen to the word. Read the word.
Draw a circle around the same word.

1.	girl	gift	game	(girl)	gas
2.	house	horse	(house)	hair	hat
3.	heart	hat	head	hen	(heart)
4.	game	(game)	goat	genie	garbage
5.	hat	hair	hand	(hat)	hamburger
6.	giant	game	girl	(giant)	giraffe

Page 64

👂 Listen to the words.

🗣 Say the words.

Do the words begin with the sound /w/, /s/, or /k/?

✎ Write **W** or **C** at the beginning of each word.

1. **C** ar	2. **W** ater
3. **W** agon	4. **W** olf
5. **C** orn	6. **C** ity
7. **C** ircle	8. **C** offee

Page 65

1. Can you see a woman?	(Yes)	No	
2. Can you see a cup?	Yes	(No)	
3. Can you see a cow?	(Yes)	No	
4. Can you see a city?	(Yes)	No	
5. Can you see a wagon?	(Yes)	No	
6. Can you see a wolf?	(Yes)	No	

Page 66

👂 Listen to the words.

✎ Write the beginning sounds of the words.

Write **c**, **g**, **h**, or **w**.

1. **C** at	2. **w** oman	3. **h** orse
4. **g** iant	5. **h** ill	6. c up
7. **h** eart	8. g ym	9. **w** ater
10. **g** iant	11. **w** atch	12. **h** ouse
13. c ircle	14. c ow	15. c ard
16. c alendar	17. c ent	18. **g** iraffe
19. c ity	20. **w** indow	21. **h** air

Page 67

👂 Listen to the sentences.

✎ Write the beginning sounds of the words.

Write **c**, **g**, **h**, or **w**.

1. The **g** irl is looking at a **g** ame.

2. The **g** iant is looking at a **g** enie.

3. The **W** oman is looking at a **C** oat.

4. The **C** at is looking at a **h** amburger.

5. The **C** ow is looking at some **W** ater.

Panel 1 (top left)

👂 Listen and ✏ Write

👂 Listen to the words.

🗣 Say the words.

Do the words begin with the sound /k/ or /y/?

✏ Write **k** or **y** at the beginning of each word.

1. **k** itten 	2. **y** o-yo 
3. **k** ettle 	4. **k** ey 
5. **y** ard 	6. **y** am 
7. **k** iss 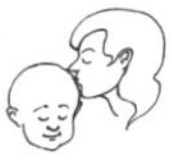	✓

Unit 10   ESL Phonics for All Ages   Book 1   © Elizabeth Claire 2007   Page **70**

Panel 2 (top right)

👂 Listen and ✏ Write

👂 Listen to the words.

🗣 Say the words.

Do you hear the sound /th/ or /ch/ ?

✏ Write **th** or **ch** at the beginning of the words.

1. **ch** air 	2. **th** umb 
3. **th** irty 30	4. **th** ousand 1,000
5. **ch** icken 	6. **ch** ildren 
7. **th** ermometer 	✓

Page **74**   ESL Phonics for All Ages   Book 1   © Elizabeth Claire 2007   Unit 11

Panel 3 (bottom left)

👂 Listen and ✏ Write

👂 Listen to the words.

🗣 Say the words.

Do you hear the sound /th/, /ch/ or /kw/ ?

✏ Write **th**, **ch**, or **qu** at the beginning of the words.

1. **ch** eek 	 2. **Th** ursday
3. **qu** een 	4. **th** irteen 13
5. **ch** eck 	6. **ch** eese 
7. **qu** art 	8. **qu** iz 

Unit 11   ESL Phonics for All Ages   Book 1   © Elizabeth Claire 2007   Page **78**

Panel 4 (bottom right)

👂 Listen and ✏ Write

👂 Listen to the words.

✏ Write the beginning sounds of the words.

Use **th**, **ch**, or **qu**.

1. **ch** ildren	2. **qu** een	3. **th** irty
4. **qu** art	5. **ch** air	6. **ch** eek
7. **th** ousand	8. **ch** erries	9. **th** umb
10. **ch** icken	11. **qu** arter	12. **qu** ilt
13. **qu** iz	14. **th** ief	15. **th** irteen
16. **ch** eck	17. **qu** estion	18. **th** ermometer

Page **79**   ESL Phonics for All Ages   Book 1   © Elizabeth Claire 2007   Unit 11

Listen and ✎ Write

👂 Listen to the words.

🗣 Say the words.

Do you hear the sound /sh/ or /wh/ ?

✎ Write **sh** or **wh** at the beginning of the words.

1. **sh** irt		2. **wh** eel	
3. **sh** oe		4. **wh** ale	
5. **wh** isker		6. **sh** ark	
7. **wh** ip		8. **wh** istle	

📖 Read and 🔍 Find

📖 Read the sentences.

🔍 Find the things in the picture. Write the number.

1. Where's the whistle?
   It's number **6**.
2. Where's the shoe?
   It's number **4**.

3. Where's the shirt?
   It's number **5**.
4. Where's the whale?
   It's number **3**.

5. Where's the shark?
   It's number **2**.
6. Where's the wheel?
   It's number **1**.

👓 Look and ✎ Write

👓 Look at the pictures.

🗣 Say the words.

What is the beginning sound?

✎ Write the letter at the beginning of each word.

1. **b** ox		2. **t** able	
3. **s** ock		4. **n** ose	
5. **c** ar		6. **r** uler	
7. **p** ants		8. **j** ar	

👓 Look and ✎ Write

👓 Look at the pictures.

🗣 Say the words.

What is the beginning sound?

✎ Write the letter at the beginning of each word.

1. **f** ish		2. **d** oor	
3. **m** oney		4. **l** unch	
5. **v** an		6. **z** ipper	
7. **g** ym		8. **g** irl	

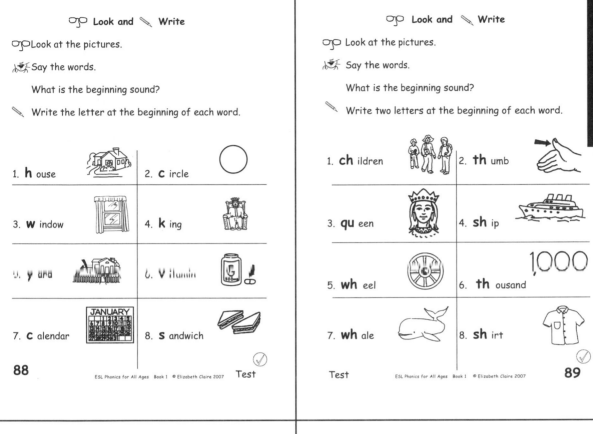

👓 Look and ✎ Write

👓 Look at the pictures.

🐞 Say the words.

What is the beginning sound?

✎ Write the letter at the beginning of each word.

1. **h** ouse	2. **c** ircle
3. **w** indow	4. **k** ing
5. **y** ard	6. **v** itamin
7. **c** alendar	8. **s** andwich

88

ESL Phonics for All Ages Book 1 © Elizabeth Claire 2007

Test

👓 Look and ✎ Write

👓 Look at the pictures.

🐞 Say the words.

What is the beginning sound?

✎ Write two letters at the beginning of each word.

1. **ch** ildren	2. **th** umb
3. **qu** een	4. **sh** ip
5. **wh** eel	6. **th** ousand
7. **wh** ale	8. **sh** irt

Test

ESL Phonics for All Ages Book 1 © Elizabeth Claire 2007

89

Review: Beginning Sounds

👂 Listen to the words.

What's the beginning sound?

✏️ Write the letter at the beginning of these words.

1. **b** ook	2. **c** ook	3. **l** ook
4. **m** at	5. **h** at	6. **b** at
7. **t** en	8. **h** en	9. **m** en
10. **b** ig	11. **p** ig	12. **d** ig
13. **h** am	14. **j** am	15. **y** am
16. **j** et	17. **n** et	18. **p** et
19. **m** an	20. **c** an	21. **f** an

Review: Beginning Sounds

👂 Listen to the words.

What's the beginning sound?

✏️ Write 2 letters at the beginning of these words.

1. **qu** een	2. **qu** arter	3. **th** ousand
4. **sh** irt	5. **sh** eep	6. **wh** ale
7. **wh** ere	8. **th** irty	9. **qu** iz
10. **ch** icken	11. **sh** oe	12. **qu** estion
13. **th** ink	14. **qu** art	15. **th** ank you

One? Or More than One?

👓 Look at the pictures.

👂 Listen to the words. 📦 Read the words.

✍️ Draw a circle around the correct word.

1. cat (cats)	2. cup (cups)
3. (jacket) jackets	4. (map) maps
5. sock (socks)	6. (notebook) notebooks
7. (jet) jets	8. rabbit (rabbits)

One? Or More than One?

👓 Look at the pictures.

👂 Listen to the words. 📦 Read the words.

✍️ Draw a circle around the correct word.

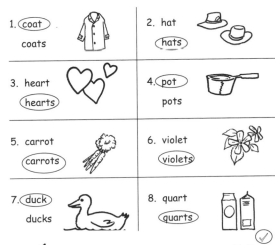

1. (coat) coats	2. hat (hats)
3. heart (hearts)	4. (pot) pots
5. carrot (carrots)	6. violet (violets)
7. (duck) ducks	8. quart (quarts)

One? Or More than One?

👓 Look at the pictures.

👂 Listen to the words.   🎁 Read the words.

✏️ Draw a circle around the correct word.

1. boy **(boys)**	2. dollar **(dollars)**
3. pen **(pens)**	4. **(teacher)** teachers
5. finger **(fingers)**	6. **(dog)** dogs
7. **(leg)** legs	8. bird **(birds)**

One? or More than One?

👂 Listen to the words

🎁 Read the words.

✏️ Draw a circle around the correct word.

1. banana **(bananas)**	2. **(toy)** toys
3. lock **(locks)**	4. **(pot)** pots
5. **(wheel)** wheels	6. chair **(chairs)**
7. shoe **(shoes)**	8. **(tiger)** tigers
9. **(duck)** ducks	10. bag **(bags)**
11. chicken **(chickens)**	12. **(boot)** boots
13. radio **(radios)**	14. **(balloon)** balloons

👂 Listen, 🗣 Say, and ✏️ Write

👂 Listen to the words.

🗣 Say the words.   Do the words end with /n/ or /l/?

✏️ Write **n** or **l** at the end of these words.

1. pai **l**	2. seve **n**
3. sai **l**	4. schoo **l**
5. poo **l**	6. fa **n**
7. pi **n**	8. ow **l**

👂 Listen, 🗣 Say, and ✏️ Write

👂 Listen to the words.

🗣 Say the words.   Do the words end with /ll/ or /k/ ?

✏️ Write **ll** or **ck** at the end of these words.

1. do **ll**	2. so **ck**
3. hi **ll**	4. be **ll**
5. tru **ck**	6. du **ck**
7. ba **ll**	8. ba **ck**

🎲 Read and 🔍 Find: Street Signs

👂 Find these words. ✏️ Write the numbers in the circles.

1. gas
2. keep off the grass
3. stop
4. one way
5. pizza

6. closed
7. open
8. motel
9. bus stop
10. no parking

👂 Listen, 🐝 Say, and ✏️ Write

👂 Listen to the words. 🐝 Say the words.
Do the words end in /p/ or /t/?

✏️ Write **p** or **t** at the end of these words.

1. roo **t**	2. ca **p**
3. soa **p**	4. nu **t**
5. ha **t**	6. je **t**
7. mo **p**	8. cu **p**

Book 2

👂 Listen, 🐝 Say, and ✏️ Write

👂 Listen to the words. 🐝 Say the words.
What sound is at the end of these words?

✏️ Write **n, l, p,** or **t** at the end of these words.

1. su **n**	2. ca **p**	3. ca **t**	4. ca **n**
5. schoo **l**	6. pe **t**	7. poo **l**	8. lio **n**
9. po **t**	10. sto **p**	11. stree **t**	12. quee **n**
13. te **n**	14. jacke **t**	15. ma **p**	16. chicke **n**
17. cu **p**	18. foo **t**	19. nigh **t**	20. soa **p**

👂 Listen, 🐝 Say, and ✏️ Write

👂 Listen to the words. 🐝 Say the words.
Do the words end in /m/ or /r/?

✏️ Write **m** or **r** at the end of these words.

1. dru **m**	2. ar **m**
3. ea **r**	4. chai **r**
5. pape **r**	6. gu **m**
7. bea **r**	8. flowe **r**

Top Left (Page 31)

🎧 Listen, 🗣 Say, and ✏️ Write

🎧 Listen to the words. 🗣 Say the words.
What sound is at the end of these words?

✏️ Write **m, r, p,** or **t** at the end of these words.

1. ma **p**	2. mo **m**
3. doo **r**	4. boa **t**
5. ha **t**	6. sou **p**
7. chai **r**	8. dru **m**

Top Right (Page 33)

🎧 Listen, 🗣 Say, and ✏️ Write

🎧 Listen to the words. 🗣 Say the words.
What sound is at the end of these words?

✏️ Write **m, l, r,** or **n** at the end of these words.

1. pe **n**	2. mai **l**
3. woma **n**	4. ar **m**
5. pape **r**	6. far **m**
7. trai **n**	8. schoo **l**

Bottom Left (Page 34)

🎧 Listen, 🗣 Say and ✏️ Write

🎧 Listen to the words. 🗣 Say the words.
What sound is at the end of these words?

✏️ Write **m, l, r,** or **n** at the end of these words.

1. schoo **l**	2. su **n**	3. sta **r**	4. mo **m**
5. tai **l**	6. pe **n**	7. poo **l**	8. lio **n**
9. dru **m**	10. wate **r**	11. mai **l**	12. quee **n**
13. te **n**	14. ca **r**	15. ma **n**	16. chicke **n**
17. tea **m**	18. roo **m**	19. doo **r**	20. fou **r**

Bottom Right (Page 35)

👆 Find and ✏️ Circle

🎲 Read the words.

✏️ Draw a circle around the same word.

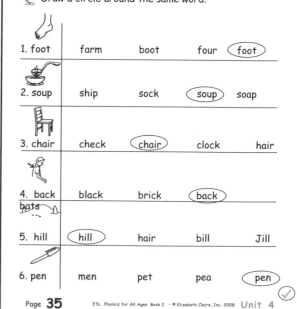

1. foot	farm	boot	four	(foot)
2. soup	ship	sock	(soup)	soap
3. chair	check	(chair)	clock	hair
4. back bats	black	brick	(back)	
5. hill	(hill)	hair	bill	Jill
6. pen	men	pet	pea	(pen)

Top Left Panel

👂 Listen, 🗣 Say, and ✏ Write

👂 Listen to the words. 🗣 Say the words.

✏ Do the words end in /b/ or /g/?

Write **b** or **g** at the end of these words.

 1. le **g**	 2. ba **g**
 3. bu **g**	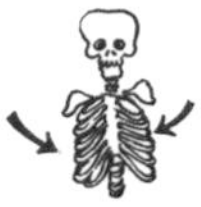 4. ri **b**
 5. cra **b**	 6. ca **b**
 7. bul **b**	 8. pi **g**

Top Right Panel

👂 Listen, 🗣 Say, and ✏ Write

👂 Listen to the words. 🗣 Say the words.
Do the words end in /d/ or /f/?

✏ Write **d** or **f** at the end of these words.

1. hal **f** 	2. be **d** 
3. roo **f** 	4. wol **f** 
 5. see **d**	 6. hea **d**
 7. clou **d**	 8. gol **f**

Bottom Left Panel

👂 Listen, 🗣 Say, and ✏ Write

👂 Listen to the words. 🗣 Say the words.
What sound is at the end of these words?

✏ Write **d**, **f**, **b**, or **g**.

 1. hea **d**	 2. pi **g**
 3. roo **f**	 4. we **b**
5. lea **f** 	6. be **d** 
7. ca **b** 	8. wol **f** 

Bottom Right Panel

👁 Find and ✂ Circle

📦 Read the words.

✏ Draw a circle around the same word.

 1. crab	cab	crib	rob	(crab)	crow
 2. bag	big	dog	bed	gab	(bag)
 3. hoof	roof	(hoof)	book	hoot	house
 4. half	wolf	head	hoof	(half)	walk
5. chief	check	leaf	cloud	(chief)	chicken
 6. frog	fog	flag	gold	golf	(frog)

Panel 1 (Top Left)

👂 Listen to the words. 🗣 Say the words.

✏ Write **x**, **ss**, or **ng** at the end of these words.

1. si **x** 		2. gra **ss** 	
3. cla **ss** 		4. a **x** 	
5. bo **x** 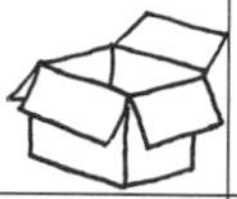		6. ki **ss** 	
7. dre **ss** 		8. ri **ng** 	✓

Panel 2 (Top Right)

👂 Listen to the words.

🗣 Say the words.

✏ Write **sh** or **th** at the end of these words.

1. mou **th** 		2. bru **sh** 	
3. fi **sh** 		4. ba **th** 	
5. wa **sh** 		6. tee **th** 	
7. di **sh** 		8. ma **th** 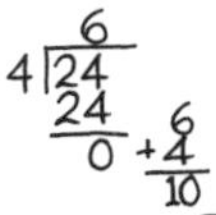	✓

Panel 3 (Bottom Left)

👂 Listen to the words.

🗣 Say the words.

✏ Write **th** or **ch** at the end of these words.

1. tee **th** 		2. chur **ch** 	
3. mou **th** 		4. in **ch** 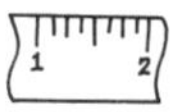	
5. ma **th** 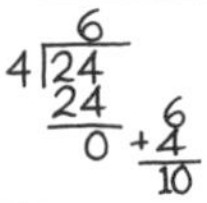		6. ba **th** 	
7. lun **ch** 		8. pea **ch** 	✓

Panel 4 (Bottom Right)

👂 Listen to the words. 🗣 Say the words.
Do the words end in /ch/, /sh/, or /th/?

✏ Write **ch**, **sh**, or **th** at the end of these words.

1. tee **th** 		2. chur **ch** 	
3. di **sh** 		4. ba **th** 	
5. ma **th** 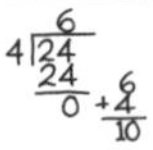		6. bru **sh** 	
7. lun **ch** 		8. in **ch** 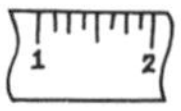	✓

Panel 1 (Page 59)

📖 Read, ✋ Find, and ✏ Circle

📖 Read the words.
✋ Find two words that are the same.
✏ Draw a circle around the same words.

1. beach (bush) push brush (bush) _____

2. mash maps (math) mouth (math) _____

3. church cloth (porch) (porch) catch _____

4. peach path (push) beach (push) _____

5. fish (fourth) (fourth) dish wash _____

6. bath math (path) beach (path) _____

Panel 2 (Page 62)

🎧 Listen, 🗣 Say, and ✏ Write

🎧 Listen to the words.
🗣 Say the words.
✏ Write **dge** or **tch** in these words.

1. bri **dge**

2. ca **tch**

3. pi **tch**

4. ju **dge**

5. wa **tch**

6. ple **dge**

7. ba **dge**

8. ma **tch**

Book 2

Panel 3 (Page 63)

👐 Read and ✏ Circle

📖 Read the words.
✋ Find two words that are the same.
✏ Draw a circle around the same words.

1. cat (rat) car cap (rat) coat _____

2. man mom (map) (map) cap mask _____

3. ball bag (bus) box boy (bus) _____

4. bread (bridge) badge brush hedge (bridge) _____

5. (kiss) king (kiss) class miss kitten _____

6. pitch (watch) patch catch (watch) crutch _____

Panel 4 (Page 68)

The Fox and the Goat

fox

water

goat

back

well

leap

📖 Read the sentences.
✏ Draw a circle around the best word.

1. One day a fox fell into a deep _____.

((well) bell)

2. "Is the water _____?" asked the goat.

(deep (good))

3. "Come down and drink," said the _____.
(goat (fox))

The Fox and the Goat

4. "We _____ get out of this well," said the fox.

   (can (cannot))

5. "Let me jump on your _____." said the fox.

   ((back) bed)

6. The goat said _____.

   ((OK) no)

7. The _____ ran away.

   (ox (fox))

8. The _____ was in the well for a very long time.

   ((goat) girl)

The Fox and the Goat

Who said it, the fox or the goat?

1. "Is the water good?"   fox   (goat)

2. "Come down and have a drink." (fox)   goat

3. "Let me jump on your back."   (fox)   goat

4. "How will I get out now?"   fox   (goat)

5.   before you leap.   (Look)   Book)

Read and Write the Number

What happened first? What happened next?

Write 1, 2, 3, 4, and 5 in the correct order.

4 The fox jumped out of the well.

2 The goat jumped into the well.

1 A fox fell into a well.

5 The fox ran away.

3 The fox jumped on the back of the goat.

The Mice, the Cat, and the Bell

mouse   mice

cat   bell

Read the sentences.

Draw a circle around the best answer.

1. A big cat liked to eat _____ .

   (rice (mice))

2. The mice were afraid of the _____ .

   (can   (cat))

3. The mice had a _____ meeting.

   ((big)   pig)

4. "The cat can _____ us because we
   cannot hear him."

   (kill) kiss)

5. "We can put a _____ on the cat," said
   one little mouse.

   (bat   (bell))

6. "Then we can hear the cat. We can _____ away."

   ((run) rug)

7. A big mouse said, "And who will _____ the bell on
   the cat?"

   (eat   (put))

8. It was easy to say, _____ not easy to do.

   (but) put)

Review 1: Ending Sounds

👂 Listen to the words. 🐝 Say the words.

✏️ Write the letter at the end of these words.

1. ma **p**	2. ca **t**	3. bu **g**
4. be **g**	5. do **g**	6. jo **b**
7. hoo **f**	8. boo **k**	9. poo **l**
10. ar **m**	11. le **g**	12. cu **t**
13. sta **r**	14. si **x**	15. ra **t**
16. brea **d**	17. cra **b**	18. bi **g**
19. gir **l**	20. sou **p**	21. ga **s**

Book 2

Review 2: Ending Sounds

👂 Listen to the words.

✏️ Write two letters at the end of these words.

1. ma **th**	2. fi **sh**	3. si **ng**
4. wa **sh**	5. pea **ch**	6. gra **ss**
7. ba **th**	8. lun **ch**	9. four **th**
10. di **sh**	11. mou **th**	12. pun **ch**
13. ba **ck**	14. ki **ng**	15. clo **th**
16. cla **ss**	17. bri **ck**	18. swi **ng**
19. che **ck**	20. ki **ss**	21. tru **ck**

Review 3: Ending Sounds

👂 Listen to the words.

✏️ Write three letters at the end of these words.

1. ma **tch**	2. he **dge**	3. ba **dge**
4. ca **tch**	5. cru **tch**	6. pi **tch**
7. sti **tch**	8. ju **dge**	9. i **tch**
10. bri **dge**	11. le **dge**	12. smu **dge**
13. ple **dge**	14. wa **tch**	15. e **dge**

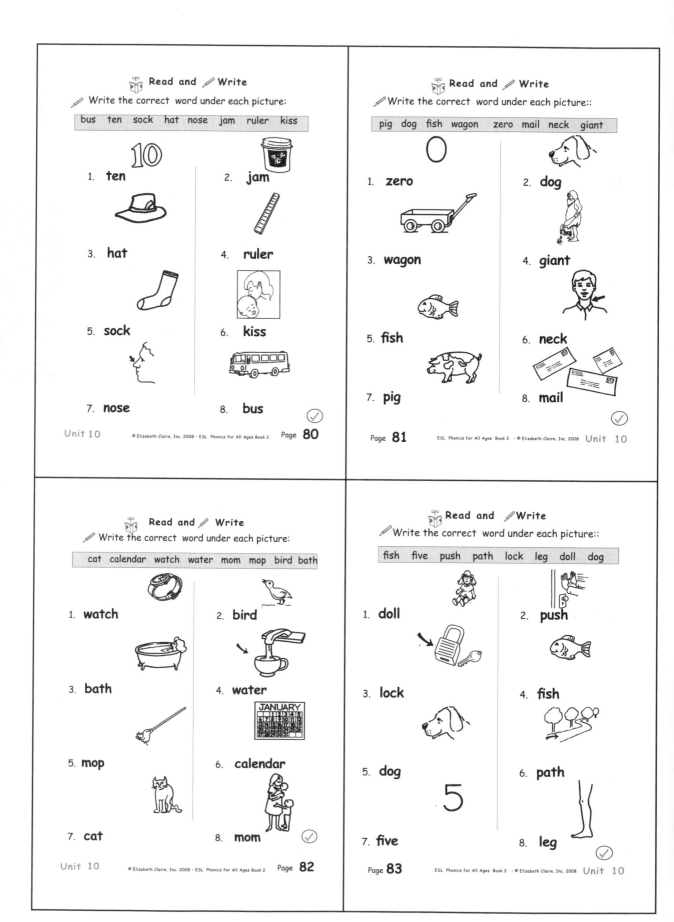

Read and Write

Write the correct word under each picture:

bus   ten   sock   hat   nose   jam   ruler   kiss

1. **ten**
2. **jam**
3. **hat**
4. **ruler**
5. **sock**
6. **kiss**
7. **nose**
8. **bus**

Read and Write

Write the correct word under each picture::

pig   dog   fish   wagon   zero   mail   neck   giant

1. **zero**
2. **dog**
3. **wagon**
4. **giant**
5. **fish**
6. **neck**
7. **pig**
8. **mail**

Read and Write

Write the correct word under each picture:

cat   calendar   watch   water   mom   mop   bird   bath

1. **watch**
2. **bird**
3. **bath**
4. **water**
5. **mop**
6. **calendar**
7. **cat**
8. **mom**

Read and Write

Write the correct word under each picture::

fish   five   push   path   lock   leg   doll   dog

1. **doll**
2. **push**
3. **lock**
4. **fish**
5. **dog**
6. **path**
7. **five**
8. **leg**

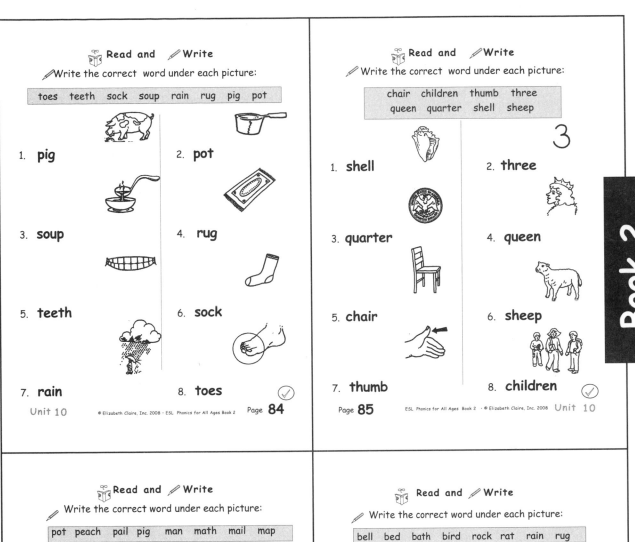

🔖 Read and ✏️ Write
✏️ Write the correct word under each picture:

toes	teeth	sock	soup	rain	rug	pig	pot

1. **pig**

2. **pot**

3. **soup**

4. **rug**

5. **teeth**

6. **sock**

7. **rain**

8. **toes**

🔖 Read and ✏️ Write
✏️ Write the correct word under each picture:

chair	children	thumb	three
queen	quarter	shell	sheep

1. **shell**

3

2. **three**

3. **quarter**

4. **queen**

5. **chair**

6. **sheep**

7. **thumb**

8. **children**

Book 2

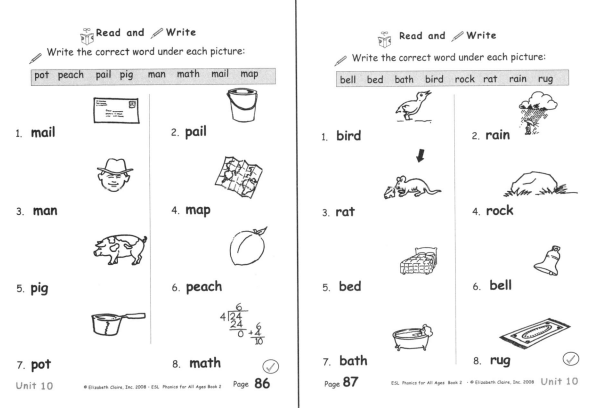

🔖 Read and ✏️ Write
✏️ Write the correct word under each picture:

pot	peach	pail	pig	man	math	mail	map

1. **mail**

2. **pail**

3. **man**

4. **map**

5. **pig**

6. **peach**

7. **pot**

8. **math**

$$4\overline{)24}$$

🔖 Read and ✏️ Write
✏️ Write the correct word under each picture:

bell	bed	bath	bird	rock	rat	rain	rug

1. **bird**

2. **rain**

3. **rat**

4. **rock**

5. **bed**

6. **bell**

7. **bath**

8. **rug**

Read and Write

Write the correct word under each picture:

game	gas	gum	goat	horse	hand	hair	hoof

1. **gum**

2. **hoof**

3. **game**

4. **hand**

5. **goat**

6. **hair**

7. **horse**

8. **gas**

© Elizabeth Claire, Inc. 2008 · ESL Phonics for All Ages Book 2

Read and Write

Write the correct word under each picture:

jet	jam	jar	jug	yard	yarn	yo-yo	yak

1. **yo-yo**

2. **yard**

3. **jet**

4. **jug**

5. **yak**

6. **jar**

7. **jam**

8. **yarn**

ESL Phonics for All Ages Book 2 · © Elizabeth Claire, Inc. 2008

Top-left panel

👂 Listen, 🗣️ Say, and ✏️ Write

👂 Listen to the words. 🗣️ Say the words.

✏️ Write **cl**, **fl**, or **pl**.

1. **cl** ock

2. **pl** ate

3. **fl** ower

4. **pl** ane

5. **cl** oud

6. **cl** othes

7. **cl** ass

8. **fl** oor

Top-right panel

👂 Listen, 🔍 Find, and ✂️ Circle

👂 Listen to the word.

🔍 Find two words that are the same.

✂️ Draw a circle around the two words.

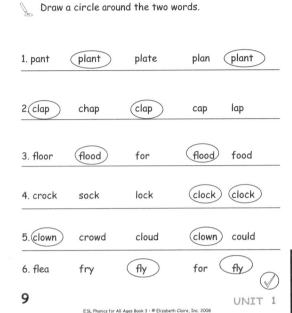

1. pant   (plant)   plate   plan   (plant)

2. (clap)   chap   (clap)   cap   lap

3. floor   (flood)   for   (flood)   food

4. crock   sock   lock   (clock)   (clock)

5. (clown)   crowd   cloud   (clown)   could

6. flea   fry   (fly)   for   (fly)   ✓

Bottom-left panel

👓 Look, 👂 Listen and 🔍 Find

👓 Look at the picture.   👂 Listen to the sentences.

🔍 Find the correct sentence.

1. 
   a. Please pass the plate.
   b. Please clap for the clown.

2. 
   a. Please fly the plane.
   b. Please close the closet.

3. 
   a. Please clean the clothes.
   b. Please sleep on the floor.

4. 
   c. Please play the flute.
   d. Please pay for the clock.

Bottom-right panel

👂 Listen, 🗣️ Say, and ✏️ Write

👂 Listen to the words. 🗣️ Say the words.

✏️ Write **bl**, **gl**, or **sl** at the beginning of the words.

1. **gl** ove

2. **sl** eeve

3. **sl** eep

4. **bl** ouse

5. **gl** asses

6. **sl** ipper

7. **bl** ock

8. **bl** anket   ✓

Book 3

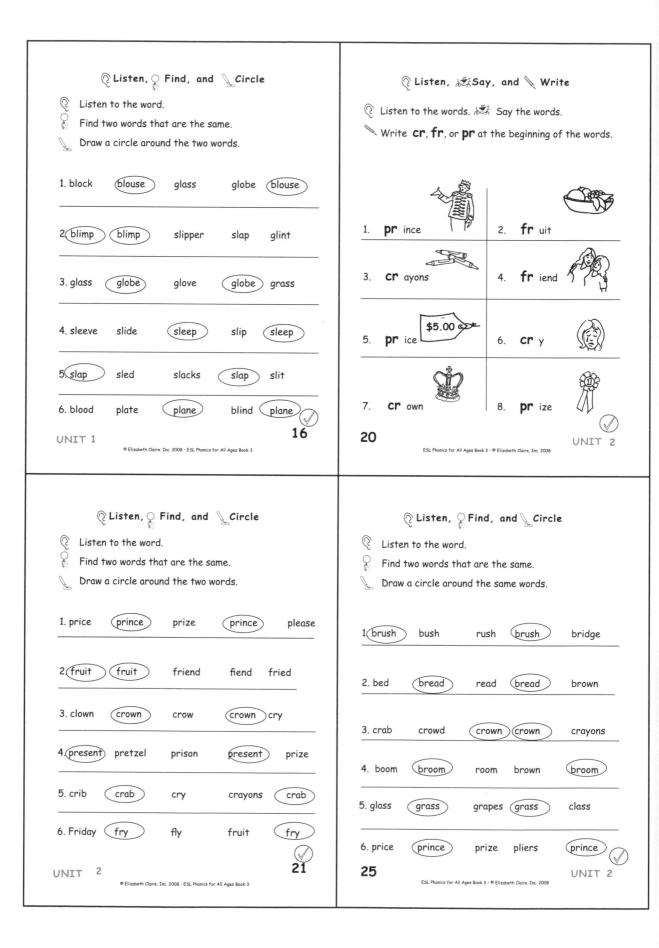

Listen, Find, and Circle

🎧 Listen to the word.
👁 Find two words that are the same.
✏️ Draw a circle around the two words.

1. block   (blouse)   glass   globe   (blouse)

2. (blimp   blimp)   slipper   slap   glint

3. glass   (globe)   glove   (globe)   grass

4. sleeve   slide   (sleep)   slip   (sleep)

5. (slap)   sled   slacks   (slap)   slit

6. blood   plate   (plane)   blind   (plane) ✓

UNIT 1   **16**

Listen, Say, and Write

🎧 Listen to the words. 🗣 Say the words.
✏️ Write **cr**, **fr**, or **pr** at the beginning of the words.

1. **pr** ince   2. **fr** uit

3. **cr** ayons   4. **fr** iend

5. **pr** ice   6. **cr** y

7. **cr** own   8. **pr** ize ✓

20

UNIT 2

Listen, Find, and Circle

🎧 Listen to the word.
👁 Find two words that are the same.
✏️ Draw a circle around the two words.

1. price   (prince)   prize   (prince)   please

2. (fruit   fruit)   friend   fiend   fried

3. clown   (crown)   crow   (crown) cry

4. (present)   pretzel   prison   (present)   prize

5. crib   (crab)   cry   crayons   (crab)

6. Friday   (fry)   fly   fruit   (fry) ✓

UNIT 2   **21**

Listen, Find, and Circle

🎧 Listen to the word.
👁 Find two words that are the same.
✏️ Draw a circle around the same words.

1 (brush)   bush   rush   (brush)   bridge

2. bed   (bread)   read   (bread)   brown

3. crab   crowd   (crown)(crown)   crayons

4. boom   (broom)   room   brown   (broom)

5. glass   (grass)   grapes   (grass)   class

6. price   (prince)   prize   pliers   (prince) ✓

25

UNIT 2

Page 26

👂 Listen to the words. 🗣 Say the words.

✒ Write **br**, **dr**, or **gr** at the beginning of the words.

1. **br** idge
2. **dr** ive
3. **dr** ess
4. **gr** ass
5. **br** ead
6. **gr** apes
7. **gr** andfather
8. **dr** um

Page 28

👂 Listen, 🗣 Say, and ✒ Write

👂 Listen to the words. 🗣 Say the words.

✒ Write **cl**, **cr**, **fl**, **fr**, **gl**, or **gr**.

1. **cl** oud
2. **cr** owd
3. **fr** y
4. **fl** y
5. **gr** ass
6. **gl** ass
7. **fl** ute
8. **fr** uit

Book 3

Page 29

🔍 Look, 👂 Listen and 🔎 Find

🔍 Look at the picture. 👂 Listen to the sentences.
🔎 Find the correct sentence.

1.
   a. The frog is frozen.
   b. The crayons are broken.

2.
   a. A fish is frying.
   b. A plane is flying.

3.
   a. She's driving a car.
   b. She's bringing a broom.

4.
   a. He's cleaning a glass.
   b. He's crossing the road.

Page 30

👂 Listen, 🗣 Say, and ✒ Write

👂 Listen to the words. 🗣 Say the words.

✒ What are the beginning sounds?

Write **br**, **cr**, **dr**, **fr**, **gr**, or **pr**.

1. **gr** ound	2. **pr** ize	3. **dr** ink
4. **fr** iend	5. **fr** y	6. **cr** y
7. **gr** andmother	8. **cr** own	9. **br** ush
10. **br** ain	11. **br** own	12. **gr** een
13. **cr** ayons	14. **fr** og	15. **pr** ince
16. **dr** um	17. **gr** ass	18. **fr** uit
19. **dr** ive	20. **dr** ess	21. **br** other

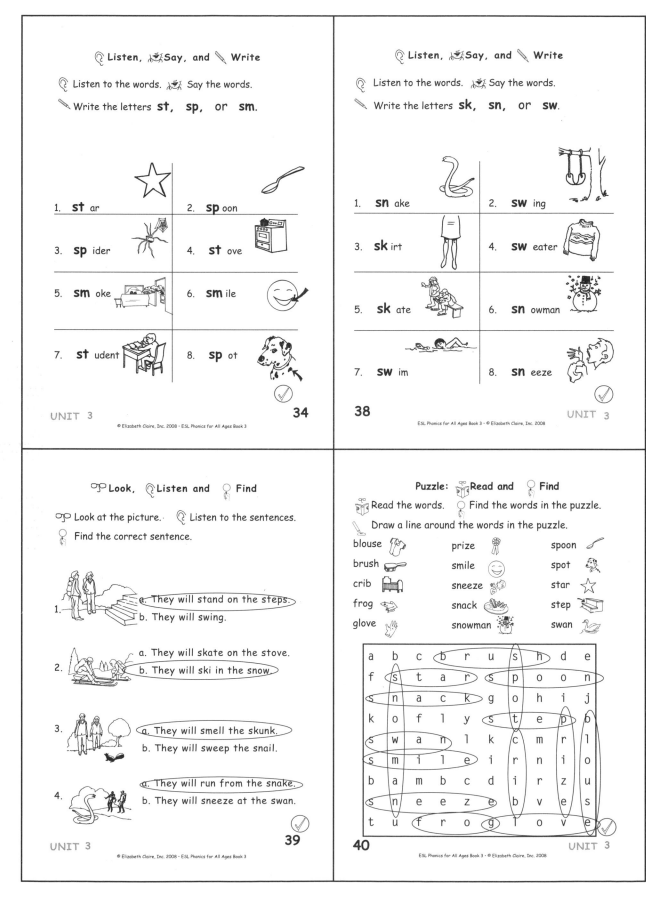

Page 34

👂 Listen, 🗣 Say, and ✏ Write

👂 Listen to the words. 🗣 Say the words.

✏ Write the letters **st, sp,** or **sm.**

1. **st** ar	2. **sp** oon
3. **sp** ider	4. **st** ove
5. **sm** oke	6. **sm** ile
7. **st** udent	8. **sp** ot

Page 38

👂 Listen, 🗣 Say, and ✏ Write

👂 Listen to the words. 🗣 Say the words.

✏ Write the letters **sk, sn,** or **sw.**

1. **sn** ake	2. **sw** ing
3. **sk** irt	4. **sw** eater
5. **sk** ate	6. **sn** owman
7. **sw** im	8. **sn** eeze

Page 39

👄 Look, 👂 Listen and 🔍 Find

👄 Look at the picture. 👂 Listen to the sentences.

🔍 Find the correct sentence.

1. a. They will stand on the steps.
   b. They will swing.

2. a. They will skate on the stove.
   b. They will ski in the snow.

3. a. They will smell the skunk.
   b. They will sweep the snail.

4. a. They will run from the snake.
   b. They will sneeze at the swan.

Page 40

Puzzle: 📦 Read and 🔍 Find

📦 Read the words. 🔍 Find the words in the puzzle.

✏ Draw a line around the words in the puzzle.

blouse   prize   spoon
brush   smile   spot
crib   sneeze   star
frog   snack   step
glove   snowman swan

a	b	c	b	r	u	s	h	d	e
f	s	t	a	r	s	p	o	o	n
s	n	a	c	k	g	o	h	i	j
k	o	f	l	y	s	t	e	p	b
s	w	a	n	l	k	c	m	r	l
s	m	i	l	e	i	r	n	i	o
b	a	m	b	c	d	i	r	z	u
s	n	e	e	z	e	b	v	e	s
t	u	f	r	o	g	l	o	v	e

Listen, Find, and Circle

👂 Listen to the word.

🔍 Find two words that are the same.

✏️ Draw a circle around the same words.

1. stamp (snack) skirt skunk (snack)

2. swan swim (snore) sweat (snore)

3. smoke (smell) (smell) spoon stamp

4. (skirt) skunk (skirt) stair star

5. snow (swan) snore sweat (swan)

6. (spider) sweater skirt spoon (spider) ✓

UNIT 3

© Elizabeth Claire, Inc. 2008 · ESL Phonics for All Ages Book 3

41

Listen, Say, and Write

👂 Listen to the words.

🗣 Say the words.

✏️ Write **sk, sl, sm, sn, sp, st,** or **sw**.

1. **sl** eep	2. **sm** ile	3. **sl** eeve
4. **sp** ot	5. **sp** oon	6. **st** ar
7. **st** ove	8. **sk** eleton	9. **sk** irt
10. **sm** oke	11. **sn** eeze	12. **sn** ake
13. **sn** ore	14. **sk** in	15. **sw** eep
16. **sm** art	17. **sw** im	18. **sn** ow
19. **st** atue	20. **st** em	21. **sp** eak

✓

42

ESL Phonics for All Ages Book 3 · © Elizabeth Claire, Inc. 2008

UNIT 3

Listen, Say, and Write

👂 Listen to the words. 🗣 Say the words.

✏️ Write **tr, tw, thr,** or **sc** at the beginning of these words.

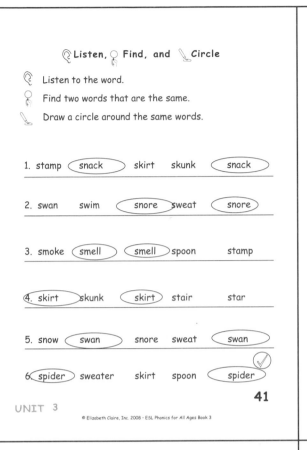

1. **tr** uck	2. **sc** ale
3. **thr** ee	4. **tr** ee
5. **tr** ain	6. **sc** hool
7. **tw** ins	8. **sc** arf

3

✓

UNIT 4

© Elizabeth Claire, Inc. 2008 · ESL Phonics for All Ages Book 3

47

Listen, Say, and Write

👂 Listen to the words.

🗣 Say the words.

✏️ Write **tr, tw, sc, st,** or **sn**.

1. **tw** inkle	2. **sc** arf	3. **sn** ake
4. **tr** ain	5. **tw** ins	6. **sn** uck
7. **sc** hool	8. **tr** uck	9. **tw** elve
10. **tw** enty	11. **tr** ash	12. **tr** ap
13. **sc** ale	14. **sn** ore	15. **tr** acks
16. **tw** eezers	17. **st** ar	18. **sc** oop
19. **tr** ay	20. **tr** ophy	21. **tw** ig

✓

49

ESL Phonics for All Ages Book 3 · © Elizabeth Claire, Inc. 2008

UNIT 4

Book 3

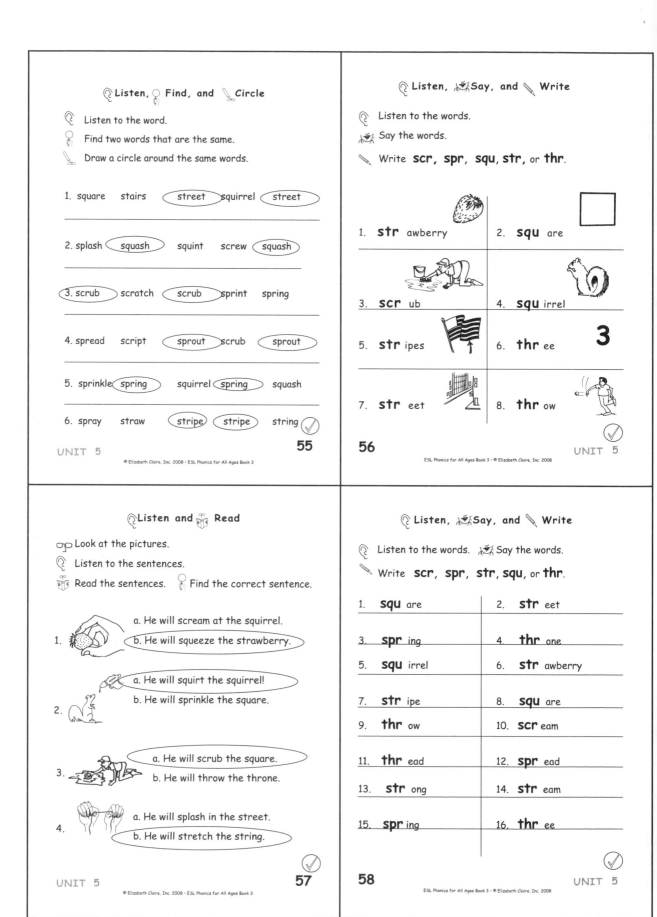

Listen, Find, and Circle

- Listen to the word.
- Find two words that are the same.
- Draw a circle around the same words.

1. square   stairs   (street)   squirrel   (street)

2. splash   (squash)   squint   screw   (squash)

3. (scrub)   scratch   (scrub)   sprint   spring

4. spread   script   (sprout)   scrub   (sprout)

5. sprinkle   (spring)   squirrel   (spring)   squash

6. spray   straw   (stripe)   (stripe)   string ✓

UNIT 5

55

© Elizabeth Claire, Inc. 2008 · ESL Phonics for All Ages Book 3

Listen, Say, and Write

- Listen to the words.
- Say the words.
- Write **scr**, **spr**, **squ**, **str**, or **thr**.

1. **str** awberry   2. **squ** are

3. **scr** ub   4. **squ** irrel

5. **str** ipes   6. **thr** ee   **3**

7. **str** eet   8. **thr** ow ✓

56

ESL Phonics for All Ages Book 3 · © Elizabeth Claire, Inc. 2008

UNIT 5

Listen and Read

- Look at the pictures.
- Listen to the sentences.
- Read the sentences. Find the correct sentence.

1. a. He will scream at the squirrel.
   (b. He will squeeze the strawberry.)

2. (a. He will squirt the squirrel!)
   b. He will sprinkle the square.

3. (a. He will scrub the square.)
   b. He will throw the throne.

4. a. He will splash in the street.
   (b. He will stretch the string.) ✓

UNIT 5

57

© Elizabeth Claire, Inc. 2008 · ESL Phonics for All Ages Book 3

Listen, Say, and Write

- Listen to the words. Say the words.
- Write **scr**, **spr**, **str**, **squ**, or **thr**.

1. **squ** are   2. **str** eet

3. **spr** ing   4. **thr** one

5. **squ** irrel   6. **str** awberry

7. **str** ipe   8. **squ** are

9. **thr** ow   10. **scr** eam

11. **thr** ead   12. **spr** ead

13. **str** ong   14. **str** eam

15. **spr** ing   16. **thr** ee ✓

58

ESL Phonics for All Ages Book 3 · © Elizabeth Claire, Inc. 2008

UNIT 5

🎧 Listen, 🐞 Say, and ✏ Write

👂 Listen to the words.

🐞 Say the words.

✏ Write **st**, **nt**, or **ft**.

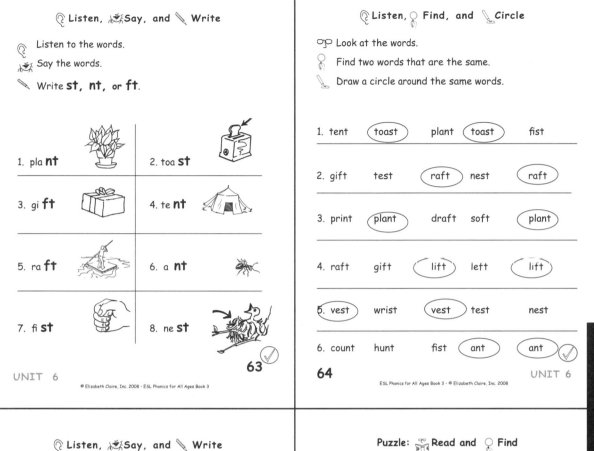

1. pla **nt**

2. toa **st**

3. gi **ft**

4. te **nt**

5. ra **ft**

6. a **nt**

7. fi **st**

8. ne **st**

🎧 Listen, 🔍 Find, and ✏ Circle

👁‍🗨 Look at the words.

🔍 Find two words that are the same.

✏ Draw a circle around the same words.

1. tent   (toast)   plant   (toast)   fist

2. gift   test   (raft)   nest   (raft)

3. print   (plant)   draft   soft   (plant)

4. raft   gift   (lift)   lett   (lift)

5. (vest)   wrist   (vest)   test   nest

6. count   hunt   fist   (ant)   (ant) ✓

🎧 Listen, 🐞 Say, and ✏ Write

👂 Listen to the words.

🐞 Say the words.

✏ Write **nk**, **nd**, or **mp**.

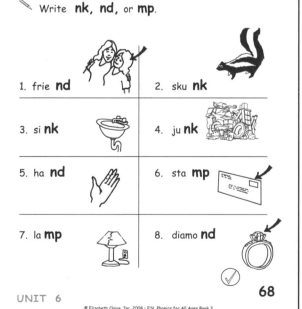

1. frie **nd**

2. sku **nk**

3. si **nk**

4. ju **nk**

5. ha **nd**

6. sta **mp**

7. la **mp**

8. diamo **nd** ✓

Puzzle: 📖 Read and 🔍 Find

📖 Read the words.   🔍 Find the words in the puzzle.

✏ Draw a circle around the words in the puzzle.

apple   little   people
bicycle   middle   puddle
bottle   needle   saddle
bubble   noodle   title
circle   paddle   turtle
juggle

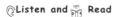

Look at the pictures.   Listen to the sentences.

Read the sentences.

Find the correct sentence.

1.
   a. There is an apple in the bottle.
   b. (There is a candle on the table.)

2.
   a. (There is a turtle in a puddle.)
   b. There is a buckle on the saddle

3.
   a. (There is a kettle on the stove.)
   b. There is a noodle on a bicycle.

4.
   a. (There is a dimple on her cheek.)
   b. There is a pimple on her nose.

74

Listen, Say, and Write

Listen to the words.   Say the words.

Write **ft, le, mp, nd, nk, nt, nk,** or **st.**

1. bott **le**	2. poi **nt**	3. si **nk**
4. gho **st**	5. bubb **le**	6. ha **nd**
7. pla **nt**	8. kett **le**	9. gi **ft**
10. app **le**	11. sa **nd**	12. sta **mp**
13. tru **nk**	14. dra **ft**	15. pu **mp**
16. ank **le**	17. toa **st**	18. te **nt**
19. ta **nk**	20. peop **le**	21. need **le**

75

Listen, Say, and Write

Listen to the words.   Say the words.

Write **b, t,** or **m** in the <u>middle</u> of these words.

1. ba **b** y	2. wo **m** an
3. po **t** ato	4. volley **b** all
5. fa **m** ily	6. ar **t** ist
7. el **b** ow	8. to **m** ato

76

Listen, Say, and Write

Listen to the words.

Say the words.

Write **k, p,** or **d** in the middle of these words.

1. pa **p** er	2. ra **d** io
3. bas **k** et	4. peo **p** le
5. ba **k** er	6. can **d** le
7. lea **d** er	8. wi **p** er

77

Listen, Say, and Write

Listen to the words.

Say the words.

Write **n, v,** or **s** in the middle of these words.

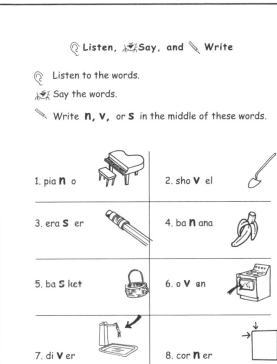

1. pia **n** o

2. sho **v** el

3. era **s** er

4. ba **n** ana

5. ba **s** ket

6. o **v** en

7. di **v** er

8. cor **n** er

78

Listen, Say, and Write

Listen to the words.

Say the words.

Write **g, l,** or **x** in the middle of these words.

1. ta **x** i

2. pi **l** ot

3. toi **l** et

4. ti **g** er

5. bo **x** er

6. alli **g** ator

7. mi **x** er

8. wa **g** on

Listen, Say, and Write

Listen to the words. Say the words.

Write **ch, sh,** or **th** in the middle of these words.

1. fea **th** er

2. ker **ch** ief

3. wa **sh** er

4. mo **th** er

5. bro **th** er

6. fa **th** er

7. cat **ch** er

8. tea **ch** er

80

Listen, Say, and Write

Listen to the words. Say the words.

Write **bb, dd, ll, mm,** or **zz** in the middle of these words.

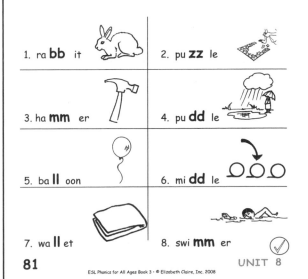

1. ra **bb** it

2. pu **zz** le

3. ha **mm** er

4. pu **dd** le

5. ba **ll** oon

6. mi **dd** le

7. wa **ll** et

8. swi **mm** er

Book 3

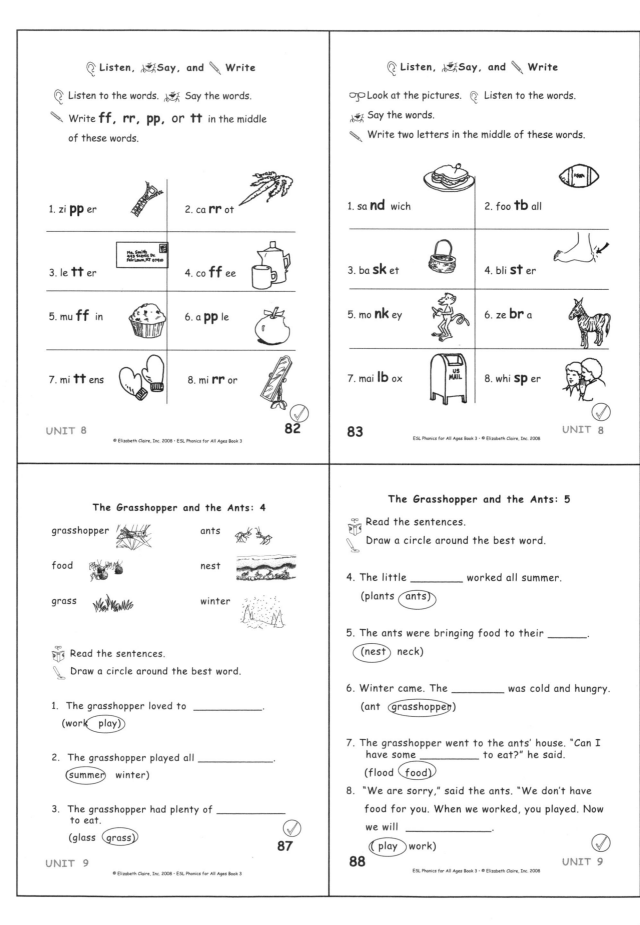

Listen, Say, and Write

Listen to the words. Say the words.

Write **ff, rr, pp,** or **tt** in the middle of these words.

1. zi **pp** er	2. ca **rr** ot
3. le **tt** er	4. co **ff** ee
5. mu **ff** in	6. a **pp** le
7. mi **tt** ens	8. mi **rr** or

© Elizabeth Claire, Inc. 2008 · ESL Phonics for All Ages Book 3

Listen, Say, and Write

Look at the pictures. Listen to the words.

Say the words.

Write two letters in the middle of these words.

1. sa **nd** wich	2. foo **tb** all
3. ba **sk** et	4. bli **st** er
5. mo **nk** ey	6. ze **br** a
7. mai **lb** ox	8. whi **sp** er

ESL Phonics for All Ages Book 3 · © Elizabeth Claire, Inc. 2008

The Grasshopper and the Ants: 4

grasshopper	ants
food	nest
grass	winter

Read the sentences.

Draw a circle around the best word.

1. The grasshopper loved to _____.
   (work (play))

2. The grasshopper played all _____.
   ((summer) winter)

3. The grasshopper had plenty of _____ to eat.
   (glass (grass))

© Elizabeth Claire, Inc. 2008 · ESL Phonics for All Ages Book 3

The Grasshopper and the Ants: 5

Read the sentences.

Draw a circle around the best word.

4. The little _____ worked all summer.
   (plants (ants))

5. The ants were bringing food to their _____.
   ((nest) neck)

6. Winter came. The _____ was cold and hungry.
   (ant (grasshopper))

7. The grasshopper went to the ants' house. "Can I have some _____ to eat?" he said.
   (flood (food))

8. "We are sorry," said the ants. "We don't have food for you. When we worked, you played. Now we will _____."
   ((play) work)

ESL Phonics for All Ages Book 3 · © Elizabeth Claire, Inc. 2008

The Grasshopper and the Ants: 6

Who said it, the grasshopper or the ants?

Draw a circle around the best word.

1. "Winter is coming." grasshopper (ants)

2. "I don't like to work." (grasshopper) ants

3. "I am cold and hungry." (grasshopper) ants

4. "Can I have some food to eat?"
    (grasshopper) ants

5. "We don't have food for you."
    grasshopper (ants)

6. "Now we will play." grasshopper (ants)

UNIT 9

89

© Elizabeth Claire, Inc. 2008 · ESL Phonics for All Ages Book 3

The Grasshopper and the Ants: 7

What happened first? What happened next?

Write 1, 2, 3, 4 and 5 in the correct order.

2 Winter came. The grass died.

5 The ants closed their door.

1 The grasshopper played all summer.

3 The grasshopper was hungry.

4 The grasshopper went to the ants' nest.

90

ESL Phonics for All Ages Book 3 · © Elizabeth Claire, Inc. 2008

UNIT 9

Book 3

Review 1: Beginning Consonant Clusters

Listen to the words. Say the words.

Write two letters at the beginning of these words.

1. **cl** oset   2. **pl** ant   3. **fl** ower

4. **pl** ane   5. **sl** eep   6. **bl** anket

7. **pr** ize   8. **br** ush   9. **fr** iend

10. **dr** ive   11. **st** ar   12. **cr** ayons

13. **sm** oke   14. **sk** irt   15. **gr** andmother

16. **tr** uck   17. **sn** ake   18. **sp** aghetti

19. **tw** enty 20. **tr** ain   21. **sw** eater

91

UNIT 10

© Elizabeth Claire, Inc. 2008 · ESL Phonics for All Ages Book 3

Review 2: Beginning Consonant Clusters

Listen to the words. Say the words.

Write three letters at the beginning of these words.

1. **scr** ub   2. **spl** ash

3. **str** ing   4. **str** awberry

5. **squ** irrel   6. **squ** are

7. **str** eet   8. **spr** inkle

9. **str** ipe   10. **squ** int

92

ESL Phonics for All Ages Book 3 · © Elizabeth Claire, Inc. 2008

UNIT 10

Review 3: Ending Consonant Clusters

👂 Listen to the words.   🗣️ Say the words.

✏️ Write two letters at the end of these words.

1. ne **st**   2. pla **nt**   3. gi **ft**

4. app **le**   5. hu **mp**   6. ju **nk**

7. bott **le**   8. sku **nk**   9. frie **nd**

10. toa **st**   11. peop **le**   12. cou **nt**

13. si **nk**   14. nood **le**   15. le **ft**

16. dri **nk**   17. sta **mp**   18. midd **le**

✓

93